Archiving Cultures

Archiving Cultures defines and models the concept of cultural archives, focusing on how diverse communities express and record their heritage and collective memory and why and how these often-intangible expressions are archival records. Analysis of oral traditions, memory texts and performance arts demonstrate their relevance as records of their communities.

Key features of this book include definitions of cultural heritage and archival heritage with an emphasis on intangible cultural heritage. Aspects of cultural heritage such as oral traditions, performance arts, memory texts and collective memory are placed within the context of records and archives. It presents strategies for reconciling intangible and tangible cultural expressions with traditional archival theory and practice and offers both analog and digital models for constructing cultural archives through examples and vignettes.

The audience includes archivists and other information workers who challenge Western archival theory and scholars concerned with interdisciplinary perspectives on tangible and intangible cultural heritage. This book is relevant to scholars involved with non-textual materials and will appeal to a range of academic disciplines engaging with "the archive".

Jeannette A. Bastian is a Professor Emerita at the School of Library and Information Science, Simmons University. A former Territorial Librarian of the United States Virgin Islands, she holds an MPhil from the University of the West Indies and a PhD from the University of Pittsburgh.

Routledge Studies in Archives
Series Editor James Lowry

Archives, Recordkeeping and Social Justice
Edited by David A. Wallace, Wendy M. Duff, Renée Saucier, and Andrew Flinn

Producing the Archival Body
Jamie A. Lee

Ghosts of Archive
Deconstructive Intersectionality and Praxis
Verne Harris

Urgent Archives
Enacting Liberatory Memory Work
Michelle Caswell

Archiving Caribbean Identity
Records, Community, and Memory
Edited by John A. Aarons, Jeannette A. Bastian, and Stanley H. Griffin

Exhibiting the Archive
Space, Encounter, and Experience
Peter Lester

The Remaking of Archival Values
Victoria Hoyle

Archiving Cultures
Jeannette A. Bastian

The following list includes only the most recent titles published within the series. A list of the full catalog of titles is available at: https://www.routledge.com/Routledge-Studies-in-Archives/book-series/RSARCH

Routledge Studies in Archives

Series Editor: James Lowry

Routledge Studies in Archives publishes new research in archival studies. Recognising the imperative for archival work in support of memory, identity construction, social justice, accountability, legal rights and historical understanding, the series extends the disciplinary boundaries of archival studies. The works in this series illustrate how archival studies intersects with the concerns and methods of, and is increasingly intellectually in conversation with, other fields.

Bringing together scholarship from diverse academic and cultural traditions and presenting the work of emerging and established scholars side by side, the series promotes the exploration of the intellectual history of archival science, the internationalisation of archival discourse and the building of new archival theory. It sees the archival in personal, economic and political activity, historically and digitally situated cultures, subcultures and movements technical and socio-technical systems, technological and infrastructural developments and in many other places.

Archival studies brings a historical perspective and unique expertise in records creation, management and sustainability to questions, problems and data challenges that lie at the heart of our knowledge about and ability to tackle some of the most difficult dilemmas facing the world today, such as climate change, mass migration, and disinformation. Routledge Studies in Archives is a platform for this work.

Archiving Cultures

Heritage, Community and the Making of Records and Memory

Jeannette A. Bastian

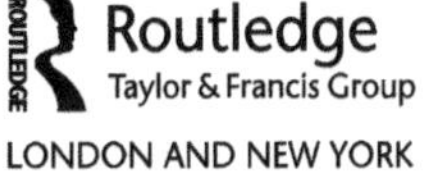

LONDON AND NEW YORK

First published 2023
by Routledge
4 Park Square, Milton Park, Abingdon, Oxon OX14 4RN

and by Routledge
605 Third Avenue, New York, NY 10158

Routledge is an imprint of the Taylor & Francis Group, an informa business

British Library Cataloguing-in-Publication Data
A catalogue record for this book is available from the British Library

ISBN: 978-0-367-54826-1 (hbk)
ISBN: 978-0-367-55071-4 (pbk)
ISBN: 978-1-003-09181-3 (ebk)

DOI: 10.4324/9781003091813

Typeset in Times New Roman
by MPS Limited, Dehradun

Contents

	Acknowledgments	viii
	Introduction: A Cultural Archive	1
1	Cultural Heritage, Archival Heritage	12
2	The Anatomy of an Archival Record	32
3	Oral Traditions and Memory Texts	52
4	Carnival in the Archives: Performance as Record	70
5	Memory, Community and Records	84
6	In the Cultural Archives	101
	Index	116

Acknowledgments

Without the encouragement of my three volunteer readers Rachel Salmond, Ross Harvey and Michael Piggott, this book may never have progressed beyond the first draft of the Introduction. Their kind but cogent critiques, their discerning eyes, their willingness to engage and most of all, their enormous generosity have been invaluable throughout this writing process. Each of them not only mentored me through it but brought their unique perspectives and specific competencies to bear – refining, suggesting and most importantly urging me to dig ever deeper into the issues. I am immeasurably grateful and thankful.

Thanks also to James Lowry, the overall editor of this Routledge archives series for his continuing support and excellent editorial suggestions as well as to the effective and efficient production team at Routledge. I am grateful as always to my life partner, Calvin F. Bastian, my fourth discerning reader, whose love and caring continues to inspire and guide me.

Introduction: A Cultural Archive

A Cultural Archives

In June 1990, representatives of the Republic of Senegal and the Territory of the United States Virgin Islands met on the National Mall in Washington, DC, a landscaped park and national space in the heart of the city. They were participants in the Smithsonian Institution's annual summer Folklife Festival organized and presented by its Center for Folklife and Cultural Heritage. The two-week-long festival featured a broad array of cultural activities and events from Senegal and the Virgin Islands. Artisans, storytellers, musicians, cooks, dancers and performers from both regions celebrated and shared their traditions. The Smithsonian Folklife Festival had already become a tradition. Started in 1967 as an "international exposition of living cultural heritage" (Smithsonian Folklife, n.d.), the annual event continues today to showcase a wide variety of cultures from around the world.

During the course of that two-week exposition, Senegalese and Virgin Islanders discovered many points of similarity between their two regions. Parallels in dance, food, music and oral traditions were sources of mutual discovery and delight. But in addition to a common African heritage, there were other connections that, while not overtly on display, bound the two regions together. Senegal and the Virgin Islands are both former colonies – one of France and one of Denmark – and both share a history of exploitation and violence through the tragedies of the slave trade.

Significantly, both cultures have relied on a blend of intangible and tangible cultural traditions for remembering and conveying their pasts as well as for conducting their presents. The mediums of transmission are primarily oral, musical and performative. Given the deeply intertwined genealogy and history that these two cultures share, their coming together was a source of knowledge and affirmation for both.

DOI: 10.4324/9781003091813-1

It celebrated heritage, cultural transference and the ongoing living reality of dynamic cultural evolution, to the extent that this event led to the inauguration of an annual folklife festival in the Virgin Islands, with Senegal participating in that first local festival on the island of St Croix in 1992.

But what if these and similar celebrations open a wider window into other complex relationships? What if these living cultural traditions, recognized as such by UNESCO in 2003, also function as the dynamic records of their communities and as the archives of their evolving history, expressed orally, musically, performatively and artifactually, rather than through text? And if they do, what then would archivists, historians, humanists, librarians, sociologists, academics and societies generally need to recognize and understand about cultural expressions and about records and their diverse forms, about their relationship to the communities that create and utilize them, and about the resilience and dynamism of archival values, so that they can place those expressions on an equal footing with those primarily textual expressions traditionally labeled as "records"? And, if these expressions are records that are as valid and legitimate as any text-based representations, how would academics, archivists and others rethink and reinterpret traditional archival understandings of records, records creation and recordkeeping[1] in order to fully embrace them?

This vignette of cultural recognition and community empowerment between the Virgin Islands and Senegal at the Smithsonian event in 1990 illustrates a small piece of the story that I wish to tell; it is part of a wider narrative of expansion, equity and inclusion in the archives.[2] Communities and societies throughout the world express and document their heritage and cultures through a broad variety of tangible and intangible forms and formats, including, but not limited to, oral traditions, performative arts, festivals, commemorations, materiality and monuments. Often not recognized as records in the traditional Western sense, these dynamic expressions in fact form the legitimate archives of a community and are critical components of documenting societies.

It is becoming increasingly clear that Western archival models, codified in the late 19th and early 20th centuries and focusing on the administrative needs of governments and institutions, have proven inadequate to fully accommodate the variety of memory and records of a global society. New models are needed to meet the demands of an international, post-colonial and decolonial environment. This book hypothesizes such a model as a cultural archives. At the heart of this hypothesis is an understanding of "archives" that considers intangible cultural expressions and tangible documentation equally as records and asks how they can be legitimately and seamlessly accommodated and subsumed within archival practice. Most importantly, what kind of framework will accommodate these cultural expressions, which are often in formats that are not generally recognized as archival? The interweaving of tangible and intangible cultural knowledge, of the archives as well as the repertoire, of the written as well as the performative – this is the archival challenge!

Historically we tend to think of archives as written, as fixed, as old and non-current, but in a cultural archives records are not fixed and static, rather they are flexible and dynamic, often embodied within people; they are responsive and adaptive to the needs of their communities. All cultures may be archiving cultures, but each culture expresses itself in highly individualistic ways. That is, every culture creates and perpetuates its own strategies for maintaining and passing on its history and its memory, for bearing evidence, and for holding its community accountable. We can call these strategies traditions and heritage, or we can call them records and archives.

One fundamental question is whether a material archival tradition can also be the appropriate vehicle for non-material expressions. I contend that the trajectory of recordmaking and keeping (stretching before and beyond the oft-cited Greek *archon*) from rock art to digital bits strongly suggests that this activity conforms to no tradition other than the human need to communicate, to record, to remember and, in both a positive and a negative sense, to control one's environment. In the 21st century, as formerly colonized and marginalized peoples, communities and nations assert their right to control their own cultures and identities, it seems clear that for archives to be globally accepted places of memory and accountability they must recognize and embrace the multiple ways – tangible and intangible, textual and oral, fixed and dynamic – in which societies document themselves.

Embracing a wide variety of non-textual forms and formats of recording within archival structures not only assists in achieving a deeper understanding of knowledge and memory production, but, importantly, establishes parity and equity in the value and significance of that knowledge and memory within the context of the community that produces it. There are many ways in which communities articulate and record themselves and "archive" their own culture and history. If archives are truly the storehouses of our collective memory, then the archives cannot be selective and choose only to store memory that conforms to a particular tradition or function within a particular framework. In order to be relevant, meaningful and enduring in a global society, the archives must be ready to represent everyone and must have the mechanisms and the strategies to do so

Definitions of "culture" tend to support this expansive and inclusive perspective. Anthropologist Clifford Geertz defined culture as "an historically transmitted pattern of meanings embodied in symbols, a system of inherited conceptions expressed in symbolic forms by means of which men communicate, perpetuate and develop their knowledge about and attitudes towards life" (Geertz, 1973, p. 89). Cultures, in this construct, form parallel streams in which each culture determines its own meanings, knowledge and symbols and methods of communicating that knowledge. Each stream is equally relevant to its particular society. In this formulation, written text may parallel oral text or performance text as cultural symbols that transmit patterns of meanings to a particular society or community. Context, or a recognition of the society from which particular patterns flow, including its recordmaking and keeping traditions, is the central key to recognizing these symbols and patterns.

Similarly, sociologist Stuart Hall defined culture in terms of shared meanings between a group, arguing that culture is not so much a set of things as a set of practices and processes: "Primarily, culture is concerned with the production and the exchange of meanings – the 'giving and taking' of meaning – between the members of a society or group" (Hall, 2013, p. xvii). These processes and these meanings may be expressed in numerous diverse ways and formats, yet be equally relevant.

This emphasis on cultural contexts is echoed in recent writings by archivists themselves. Australian Chris Colwell, referencing Michael Buckland's discussion of process, notes that "the record as process, like information as process, is situational. In each context what to record and how to record it, and indeed what is considered a record, will be different" (Colwell, 2020, p. 23). As British archival theorist, Geoffrey Yeo also observes, "Context, as so often, is all important" (Yeo, 2008, p. 141).

Why This Book?

This book is being written against a background of evolving global sensibilities to issues of social justice and archival silences. The emergence of formerly colonized entities into fully realized nations in the mid-20th century not only accelerated the questioning of the hegemony of the West but also highlighted nationalistic desires for self-determination and self-realization. The records of both colonial and precolonial pasts are heavily implicated in that quest. It is inevitable, given the history of colonization, that Western traditions have for several centuries dominated discourse in determining what constitutes an archives, and, by implication, a cultural archives.

The cultural expressions of marginalized, often non-Western societies have been either sidelined as folklore, siloed as pertaining only to specific groups, or generally relegated to the past. While there are hopeful signs that the tide is turning as the societies of former colonies increasingly establish their own voices, decolonize their history and reject imposed frameworks, the blending of all voices is still a distant, and possibly unachievable, aspiration. Nonetheless, it is an aspiration that archival practices, despite their reputation as representatives and creators of dominant narratives, can model.

The making and keeping of records have a very long history. While some historians and archeologists credit the invention of writing with the making of records and identify the clay tablets of the Assyrians (ca 2100 BCE) as the earliest effort at recordkeeping, others point to the petroglyphs and rock art of Indigenous communities thousands of years earlier as markers to record events.

Jamaican archcologist Ivor Connolley, for example, analyzing the rock art of the Taino, writes

> Pictograms, that is, drawings of a swimming turtle, a bird in flight, a crawling iguana, a glaring owl, a cautious coney, a cacique's staff, may be seen as a descriptive record of items of the early people's physical inventory, but it is more than that. Petroglyphs, that is, incisions or engravings on cave walls may also be seen as a record of a personal spiritual journey … Through these drawings, engravings and sculptures the early ethnic groups have shared with us a story of their religion … their hierarchy, their division of labour, and their political structure.
>
> (Connolley, 2018, pp. 651–652)

Through the centuries, especially as societies moved from orality to literacy, the keeping of records became a central administrative activity for governments, for policy-making, for evidence, but primarily for bureaucratic control. During the era of European conquest in the 17th, 18th and 19th centuries, recordkeeping practices were critical tools of the colonizers, not only for claiming land and creating boundaries but also for controlling populations. By the late 19th and early 20th century, Western archivists and recordkeepers were consolidating and encoding centuries, if not millennia, of archival practice into manuals that hugely influenced their archival protocols and continue to influence archival practice today.

But over several decades, and intensifying in the first two of this century, a proliferation of writings and presentations by archivists and others have advocated for change within the archives, recognizing that the structures and goals of the archives no longer respond to social needs, and, in fact, often work against them. To many of these authors and theorists, the archives is hopelessly broken because the very rationale for the archives' existence is the issue. But this perspective may be an oversimplification. The protean nature of the archives suggests that the records of oppression can also be tools against oppression, the records of control can also be means to reparations, the archives of domination are also sites for social justice. Kirsten Weld, exploring the revelations of the police archives in Guatemala, writes "archival thinking demands that we see archives not only as data to be mined by researchers but also as more than the sum of their parts – instruments of political action" (Weld, 2014, p. 13).

While changes in archival practices and attitudes have evolved and continue to evolve, the built-in paradoxes of the archives make it difficult to imagine wholesale a model for change. Nonetheless, this book explores the possibility that, despite the often oppressive and dominant nature of archival structures, reconceptualizing these structures as expanded spaces that accommodate the material and non-material, the dominant and marginalized, and the oppressive and victimized alike may frame a model for change that gives them new relevant life. And archival voices advocating the reconsideration of records within the context of the intangible and non-textual are becoming louder and more insistent, foregrounding in particular marginalized, Indigenous and formerly colonized communities. As Evelyn Wareham notes on the records of Pacific Islands communities, they are typically "stories, songs, dances, myths, and traditions passed through generations by word of mouth" – the very things that give communities identity (Wareham, 2002, p. 196).

Modeling an archival perspective that accommodates and equalizes both the textual archives and the cultural archives requires attention to a number of conceptual threads that are woven throughout these chapters. Foremost among these is defining the record itself in a way that is malleable enough to accommodate a range of markers and expressions and yet not so protean that it loses its meaning entirely. But other developments in the area of cultural heritage and of archives at the end of the 20th century suggest that an even broader understanding of documentation is needed.

These developments include the global recognition by UNESCO of Intangible Cultural Heritage and the scholarly debates that this has engendered. They include the postmodern academic archival turn, which both stretches and endangers the concept of archives. Such developments expand notions of heritage and of archives beyond the text, and complicate those notions. Additional threads importantly include postcolonialism and the subsequent reinterpretation of national heritages by formerly colonized entities, specifically in the areas of language and literacy, orality and performance, memory and artifact. Gaps in the archives, particularly those relating to marginalized and oppressed communities, increase the urgency to uncover and embrace alternate forms of records. Woven within these threads are global issues of social justice, equity and transparency – all significant factors in fashioning a holistic understanding of cultures and societies that can be harmonized with the values and principles that guide archival praxis.

Reimagining Archives

The need for new perspectives in the understanding of archives and records, together with the recognition that traditional methods no longer meet societal needs, has been growing since the turn of the 21st century. Although fueled by societal turns towards globalism and the imperatives of social justice, perhaps no factor has been more influential in driving that need than the realization within archival and academic communities of the power of archives, the non-neutrality of the record itself, and the consequences of that power and non-neutrality for all users – not only for academics and curators, but also for governments and policy-makers. The growing recognition of the injustices of imperialism and the rights of Indigenous peoples and an increasing desire by communities and groups to assert and express their identities combined with the progressively sophisticated technological affordances to do so, have all fueled a desire for awareness and acceptance of recordkeeping practices beyond the textual.

Unsettling the archives by reconceptualizing and extending archival theory not only works towards decolonizing the archives, but also enhances global cultural patrimony by embracing an expansive and inclusive understanding of records creation. As Hall pointed out, "What is important are the significant *breaks* – where old lines of thought are disrupted, older constellations displaced, and elements, old and new, are regrouped around a different set of premises and themes" (Hall, 1980, p. 57). My objective then is to reimagine those "breaks" in an archival multiverse where all forms of "record" are equally treated, to disrupt and reimagine conventions, and to regroup around premises that fold accepted theory within expanded propositions.

Documenting all peoples within the archives has long been an aspiration of archivists, who need to move beyond the boundaries of Western conventions if they are to realize those aspirations, with the affordances of technology to help. We in the 21st century have the good fortune to live in a digital age where the possibilities for linking, illuminating, showcasing and creating access to both tangible and intangible records extend as far as our imaginations will take us. In the digital realm, where scholars are already exploring the potential for presenting a wide variety of cultural assets, the possibilities for expanding the archives in tandem with those explorations offer unprecedented opportunities for redefining traditional concepts.

To emphasize the universality of recordmaking and keeping, I focus particularly on those societies outside or on the edges of primarily Western traditions that express and record their collective heritage and memory in non-textual modes; I ask why and how these expressions should be considered and treated as archival. By engaging simultaneously with both the cultural heritage and the archival disciplines, I explore and interrogate archives from a cultural heritage point of view and cultural heritage from an archives view in order to construct a framework that embraces core archival theory and an array of cultural premises. The objective is to broaden and expand the concept of "archives" beyond the boundaries of currently accepted, primarily Western, archival tradition and to present a credible case for the equal inclusion of diverse recordmaking within the archives. Through each chapter, I hope to build a theoretical framework that accommodates both conventional archival records and the many and varied unconventional ways in which communities document themselves and their cultural traditions. Far from rejecting accepted Western archival theory, I intend to analyze aspects of it to explore whether and how it can be reinterpreted and re-purposed to accommodate oral traditions and other non-textual expressions

This book is not so much an attempt to decolonize the archives as to flatten them out, to provide a level playing field for all expressions that can be considered records, to break down the archival box in which text and fixed records offer particular definitions of society, to broaden and deepen a definition of archival provenance that finds room for a flexible and expandable understanding of the creators and creations of records.

Structure of the Book

Climbing outside the archival box means building a case for inclusion of a variety of expressions to be considered archival. The first chapter expands on the core threads of the book laid out in this Introduction. It considers both cultural heritage and archival heritage and follows the developing trajectory of those definitions up to the present. It explores the ways in which theorizing about "the archive" in other disciplines has influenced and expanded a general understanding of archives, and considers how thinking about records from a cultural heritage perspective changes our understanding of what a record is and what needs to be archived.

In Chapter 2, I address the central issue of the record and offer a discussion and analysis of the Western archival and textual legacy, together with its international contextualization. I make the case for thinking beyond accepted Western archival theory and considering a wide range of community expressions as cultural records. I connect established archives and records theories with dynamic cultural expressions, demonstrating why and how these expressions might fit within archival theory. Using examples from archives and other disciplines, I suggest how the combination of archival methodology and cultural heritage methodology might enhance understanding of non-traditional records, and begin to conceptualize this methodology, the thread of which carries through subsequent chapters.

Chapters 3 through 5 each address a different aspect of cultural expression, demonstrating how each fits within an archival matrix. Chapter 3 considers orality in terms of a text and investigates ways in which a variety of cultural heritage expressions become memory texts that function both as historical records and as evidence of actual events. Chapter 4 showcases the embodied archives of performances including dance, commemorations and celebrations. Chapter 5 focuses on the records of shifting collective and cultural memory and the place of community. It addresses the archival obligation to the records of memory and how that responsibility can be fulfilled. Technology and its potential in supporting new documentary paradigms are explored in Chapter 6, which also reflects on the critical importance of thinking archivally and concludes with a final example of unity within the archives.

A Note on the Author

It would be more than presumptuous of me to speak about culture and cultural heritage without declaring my own cultural roots. My own cultural journey includes a number of watershed events, as it does for most people. A Jewish, white, female, immigrant, I came to the United States from England as a teenager with my family. As a young adult, I moved to the Caribbean – St Thomas, United States Virgin Islands – where I worked as a librarian and library administrator in public libraries and archives for over 25 years. During those years I took time off to live in Jamaica and study for an MPhil in Caribbean literature at the University of the West Indies. Reading Caribbean literature, particularly that of authors such as George Lamming and Samuel Selvon, both of whom had to leave the Caribbean to find a publisher and an audience, I began to understand the intricacies of Caribbean identity and colonial impositions. Eventually, I resumed my studies and, following a PhD at the University of Pittsburgh, taught Archives for 20 years at Simmons University in Boston, discovering a love not only for teaching but also for research and writing.

Now, a semi-retired academic, I have returned home to St Thomas and to my extended family and community. I am privileged to have been appointed Honorary Fellow at the University of the West Indies Department of Library and Information Studies, where I supervise and mentor students in the Department's nascent MPhil/PhD Program.

While my cultural orientation and my writing stems in large part from my varied exposure to living, traveling, working and studying in the Caribbean, it is also influenced by my "outsider" status as a non-West Indian and as an immigrant. Navigating one's place in a society that is not one's own requires a willingness to recognize oneself from without as well as within. Whether all these experiences qualify me to reflect on cultural heritage I cannot judge; I only know that these varied experiences have convinced me of the centrality of community, of cultural heritage, and of the critical importance of cultural acknowledgment for community and personal identity. I leave it up to the reader to make any further judgments about whether I am equipped to contribute in this space.

Notes

1 The term Recordkeeping is used throughout this book and follows American usage as found in the Society of American Archivists Dictionary, https://dictionary.archivists.org/entry/recordkeeping.html

2 According to the Society of American Archivists Dictionary, the term "archives" has at least three different meanings: It may refer to collections of historical records; it may refer to the place where these records are kept; it may refer to the practice of organizing the records to bring them into an archives. In this volume, "archives" generally refers to collections of records but, as made clear through context, may also refer to a place.

References

Colwell, C. (2020). *Records are practices, not artefacts: An exploration of recordkeeping in the Australian Government in the age of digital transition and digital continuity* [Unpublished doctoral dissertation]. University of Technology Sydney.

Connolley, I.C. (2018). Jamaican Taino symbols: Implications for regional chiefdoms and their chronology. In J.A. Bastian, J.A. Aarons & S.H. Griffin (Eds) *Decolonizing the Caribbean Record: An Archives Reader* (pp. 651–672). Litwin Books.

Geertz, C. (1973). *The interpretation of cultures: Selected essays by Clifford Geertz*. Basic Books.

Hall, S. (1980). Cultural studies: Two paradigms. *Media, Culture and Society*, 2, pp. 57–72.

Hall, S., Evans, J. & Nixon, S. (Eds.) (2013). *Representation, cultural representations and signifying practices* (2nd ed.). Sage Publications. (xvii).

Smithsonian Folklife Festival (n.d.). *Mission and history*. https://festival.si.edu/about-us/mission-and-history/smithsonian

Wareham, E. (2002). From explorers to evangelists: Archivists, recordkeeping, and remembering in the Pacific Islands. *Archival Science*, 2, pp. 187 208.

Weld, K. (2014). *Paper Cadavers: The Archives of Dictatorship in Guatemala*. Duke University Press, 13.

Yeo, G. (2008). Concepts of record (2): Prototypes and boundary objects. *The American Archivist*, 71(1), pp. 118–143.

1 Cultural Heritage, Archival Heritage

Introduction

Archives and cultural heritage are a natural pairing. The archives and records of a society form part of its cultural heritage, and the archival institutions of that society are among the social institutions charged with responsibility for documenting, preserving and making those archives and records usable. Certainly, archivists see themselves as advocates, defenders and even shapers of the cultural record. The assumptions of these simple sentences, however, give no account of the complex nature of cultural heritage and archives. Social constructions, evolving identities and political implications dictate that, inevitably, judgments and choices about cultural and archival heritages will be made and values will be weighed. While some values will be key others will be sidelined. As cultural heritage advocates and archivists attempt to establish and consolidate the legacies of the societies they work within, they also become unwitting co-conspirators in influencing what is remembered and what is forgotten.

This chapter expands on some of the core themes of this book – cultural heritage, archival heritage and the relationships between them in the formation of a cultural archive. How does archival theory support cultural heritage? How do the values of cultural heritage fit into an archival model? How have academic ways of theorizing "the archive" influenced and broadened the general understanding of records and brought a cultural heritage perspective to the fore?

When cultural expressions are placed within an archival space and archives within a cultural space, some of the tangential, though distinct, disciplines that also claim a cultural and an archival heritage are brought into consideration. Archeology, anthropology, public history, performance arts and memory studies all point to the many ways that societies value, receive and impart information, express their identities

DOI: 10.4324/9781003091813-2

and record those expressions. But, although nations, communities and individuals express and record themselves in many ways, the human values that are being expressed and recorded are essentially similar. The outward trappings may differ, but the inner humanity is shared. It is this sharing of humanity that mandates equal consideration for all ways of expressing and recording and is the concern of this book.

From Monuments to Intangible Cultural Heritage

Until recently, cultural heritage has primarily been defined through Western eyes. Often seen as a weapon of European imperialism and a "privileging of the 'written text'" (Butler, 2007, p. 39), scholars trace the beginnings of this appropriation of cultural heritage to ancient Alexandria, through the Greeks and Romans and thence to Europe. Culturalist Beverley Butler writes,

> This particular line in cultural transmission has canonised and subsequently universalised a certain tradition as the cultural 'norm'; this is a tradition synonymous not only with the possession of tangible, monumental heritage in the public sphere but also with the fixing or objectification of memory as written culture. Thus 'the text' and 'the book' are valourised over oral, memorising traditions (p. 35).

That this perspective was deeply exclusive became increasingly evident in the mid-20th century with the ebbing of colonialism and the rise of emergent nations. Nonetheless, it became the basis for definitions of cultural heritage by global entities.

As a bulwark against cultural heritage erasure, UNESCO (United Nations Educational Scientific and Cultural Organization), founded in 1945, was originally established to rebuild schools, libraries, museums and other educational and cultural institutions that had been destroyed in World War II. Recognizing that cultural heritage, both physical and conceptual, is always under siege, UNESCO's first stated mission was to build peace through international cooperation in education, sciences and culture. This mission rapidly broadened to include the defining, safeguarding and preserving of cultural heritage. Today, UNESCO's vision statement affirms that "by promoting cultural heritage and the equal dignity of all cultures, UNESCO strengthens the bonds among nations" (UNESCO in brief, n.d.).

Initially following the well-worn trajectory of privileging European cultural heritage, UNESCO's definitions of cultural heritage, contested and fiercely debated by member nations, have dramatically changed over the years. Beginning in 1954, UNESCO began a series of conferences and published conventions that refined and gradually expanded definitions of cultural heritage and developed strategies to protect that heritage.

Its first convention statement in 1954, *Convention for the Protection of Cultural Property in the Event of Armed Conflict*, recognized only tangible heritage as cultural heritage, defining it in both physical and global terms as "movable or immovable property of great importance to the cultural heritage of every people", and including the buildings designed to hold this cultural heritage, such as archives, libraries and museums (UNESCO, 1954). Examples of cultural heritage included monuments, archeological sites, works of art, manuscripts, books and other objects of artistic, historical or archeological interest, scientific collections and important collections of books or archives. Cultural heritage was tangible property physically situated in a recognized cultural heritage repository and assumed to be of universal value. It was a legacy defined by its historic or artistic value that included not only years of high European cultural traditions but also cultural artifacts acquired and appropriated from developing nations by the developed world.

Limiting cultural heritage to tangible culture reflected not only a European bias but a colonial one. Member nations outside the European sphere, including the colonized and formerly colonized, took immediate exception to this definition, lobbying extensively for the inclusion of definitions that reflected their cultures. It was a crusade that was to continue throughout the 20th century and into the 21st century. Despite these efforts, in 1972 the definition of heritage still focused on the physical and historical and was expanded only to include natural heritage. The *Convention Concerning the Protection of the World Cultural and Natural Heritage*, defined cultural heritage as, "monuments: architectural works, works of monumental sculpture and painting, elements or structures of an archeological nature, inscriptions, cave dwellings and combinations of features, which are of outstanding universal value from the point of view of history, art or science". The definition included buildings or groups of buildings whose architectural features or placement in the landscape were deemed to have universal value and certain man-made sites considered to have archeological significance (UNESCO, 1972).

In 1989, after continuing pressure from non-European member nations, the definition of cultural heritage was extended to include folklore. The *Recommendation on the Safeguarding of Traditional Culture and Folklore* reads,

> Folklore (or traditional and popular culture) is the totality of tradition-based creations of a cultural community, expressed by a group or individuals and recognized as reflecting the expectations of a community in so far as they reflect its cultural and social identity; its standards and values are transmitted orally, by imitation or by other means. Its forms are, among others, language, literature, music, dance, games, mythology, rituals, customs, handicrafts, architecture and other arts
>
> (UNESCO, 1989)

The term "folklore", however, did not resolve the issue, but continued to reflect European bias, essentially creating a second-order heritage. Pressure by non-European nations and territories continued and in 2001, UNESCO's *Universal Declaration on Cultural Diversity* recognized that,

> Culture takes diverse forms across time and space. This diversity is embodied in the uniqueness and plurality of the identities of the groups and societies making up humankind. As a source of exchange, innovation and creativity, cultural diversity is as necessary for humankind as biodiversity is for nature. In this sense, it is the common heritage of humanity and should be recognized and affirmed for the benefit of present and future generations
>
> (UNESCO, 2002)

This declaration set the stage for recognition of intangible cultural heritage on a par with the tangible, although it still took another year to make the final leap.

Nine years after Senegal and the Virgin Islands celebrated and shared their heritage on the Washington Mall, the Smithsonian's Center for Folklife and Heritage engaged with cultural heritage in a different arena. The Smithsonian convened an international forum to assess the implications of the 1989 UNESCO recommendations on the protection of traditional culture and folklore (Seitel, 2001). This conference, attended by representatives from thirty-seven countries, was a major driver for UNESCO's subsequent recognition of both material and non-material manifestations of cultural expressions.

In its 2003 adoption of the *Convention for the Safeguarding of Intangible Cultural Heritage*, UNESCO based its recommendations on a Japanese model that had been in place since the 1950s. Until 2003 UNESCO had defined cultural heritage as objects from the past, but it was now willing to recognize intangible cultural heritage as cultural practices that were both dynamic and living. In Article 2 of the Convention, it presented its new definition:

1 The "intangible cultural heritage" means the practices, representations, expressions, knowledge, skills – as well as the instruments, objects, artifacts and cultural spaces associated therewith – that communities, groups and, in some cases, individuals recognize as part of their cultural heritage. This intangible cultural heritage, transmitted from generation to generation, is constantly recreated by communities and groups in response to their environment, their interaction with nature and their history, and provides them with a sense of identity and continuity, thus promoting respect for cultural diversity and human creativity.
2 The "intangible cultural heritage", as defined in paragraph 1 above, is manifested inter alia in the following domains:

   a Oral traditions and expressions, including language as a vehicle of the intangible cultural heritage;
   b Performing arts;
   c Social practices, rituals and festive events;
   d Knowledge and practices concerning nature and the universe;
   e Traditional craftsmanship (UNESCO, *Text*, 2003).

In commenting on the shift from folklore to intangible cultural heritage, anthropologist Chiara Bortolotto points out that it represented a movement away from a European archival approach that emphasized not only history but objects fixed in time to an approach that, influenced by Japan's long tradition of safeguarding the intangible aspects of its cultural heritage, was fluid and changeable. She writes that, "The reflection on what was formerly known as 'folklore' by UNESCO was an important stage in the shift toward the idea of intangible heritage". She saw this as a movement towards a process-oriented approach following the Japanese model (Bortolotto, 2007, pp. 21–22).

In 2005, UNESCO was once again pressured to affirm its commitment to cultural diversity and expanded its 2003 recommendations in a stronger *Convention on the Protection and Promotion of the Diversity of Cultural Expressions.* This convention expanded the definition of cultural diversity to take a more holistic approach:

> 'Cultural diversity' refers to the manifold ways in which the cultures of groups and societies find expression. These expressions are passed on within and among groups and societies. Cultural

> diversity is made manifest not only through the varied ways in which the cultural heritage of humanity is expressed, augmented and transmitted through the variety of cultural expressions, but also through diverse modes of artistic creation, production, dissemination, distribution and enjoyment, whatever the means and technologies used
>
> (UNESCO, 2005)

UNESCO's most recent list of heritage categories specifies what it considers as cultural heritage:

- Tangible cultural heritage:
  - Movable cultural heritage (paintings, sculptures, coins, manuscripts)
  - Immovable cultural heritage (monuments, archeological sites and so on)
  - Underwater cultural heritage (shipwrecks, underwater ruins and cities)
- Intangible cultural heritage: oral traditions, performing arts, rituals (UNESCO. *Database*, 2003).

Central in the development of UNESCO's definition was the critical recognition that tangible and intangible heritage work in tandem. Tangible cultural heritage generally includes intangible elements and vice versa; neither stands alone. An example of this is Taino rock art, where depictions are physically etched into stone but what they represent is part of the community's orally transmitted knowledge. This interdependency was expressed by UNESCO's Assistant Director General for Culture in 2003 when the *Convention for the Safeguarding of Intangible Cultural Heritage* was first introduced. He stated that, "cultural heritage is a synchronized relationship involving society … norms and values", and suggested that the symbiotic relationship between the tangible and intangible meant that, "the intangible heritage should be regarded as the larger framework within which tangible heritage takes on shape and significance (Bouchenaki, 2003).

Nonetheless, UNESCO's division of cultural heritage into siloed categories has drawn severe criticism from those who claim that culture must be all-inclusive and that its division creates a false dichotomy. Anthropologist Máiréad Nic Craith, for example, welcomes the shift in emphasis from tangible heritage to intangible heritage, but recommends thinking about heritage in more holistic terms and, "recognising the significance of and interactions between the tangible and intangible, objects as well as cultural spaces, embracing both process and product, and placing particular emphasis on ordinary people as tradition definers and tradition bearers" (Craith, 2008, p. 57).

UNESCO's efforts to safeguard cultural heritage perpetuate these silos through the creation and maintenance of three programs that enable the annual nomination of heritage items by countries and their selection by committees. In 1972 UNESCO began listing *World Heritage Sites* in order to encourage the preservation of natural and cultural heritage that focuses on landscapes around the world (UNESCO World Heritage Center, 1992–2022). The *Memory of the World* (MOW) program, initiated in 1992, focuses on documentary heritage in a wide variety of formats from papyrus to digital files. Declaring that, "Our cultural heritage influences our collective memories", and that, "documentary heritage includes ... information that has been created and stored in a variety of ways and passed on from generation to generation" (UNESCO, *Memory,* n.d.), the program connects memory to heritage and suggests that cultural memory is embodied within the objects and artifacts themselves over time. In 2008, UNESCO established its *Lists of Intangible Cultural Heritage* (UNESCO, *Intangible*, n.d.) which seeks to showcase cultural diversity and cultural connections through intangible heritage around the world.

The paradox implicit in creating a permanent and fixed site for an impermanent and fluid heritage has been noted by many critics of the concept of intangible cultural heritage. In addition to questioning whether it is appropriate to set global criteria for community-based cultural practices, they note the incongruity of safeguarding something that is always in process. Cultural heritage scholar Marilena Alivizatou, for example, points out that, "Inherent in notions of safeguarding and preserving intangible heritage is the idea of making permanent the impermanent and therefore capturing and freezing that which is meant to appear, disappear and reappear"(Alivizatou, 2013, p. 10).

Cultural Heritage – A Broader Vision

UNESCO's definitions of cultural heritage accommodate the varied needs and demands of its member countries. Its primary focus is on safeguarding the diversity of its members' heritages by supporting them through a global imprimatur and making it clear that expressions of their heritage are universally acknowledged as benefits to humanity. While UNESCO's websites encompass an expansive human landscape, they focus on presentation and preservation, leaving broader analyses of cultural heritage to others. Stuart Hall, for example, connected heritage with community, memory and identity when he suggested that, "We should think of The Heritage as a discursive practice. It is one of the ways in which the nation slowly constructs for itself a sort of collective social memory … nations construct identities by selectively binding their chosen high points and memorable achievements into an unfolding 'national story'" (Hall, 1999–2000, p. 5).

Hall supported a comprehensive approach to cultural heritage, characterizing it as dynamic and fluid and including a wide variety of institutions and practices. He took strong exception to the propensity for only "keeping what already exists" (Hall, p. 3). Rather he saw cultural heritage as both an active and a living activity that existed together with the heritage of the past – a heritage that marginalizes no-one but includes the full diversity of the nation and the society.

In 2002 "heritage" was similarly defined as dynamic and integral to identity by the International Council of Monuments and Sites, a non-governmental organization associated with UNESCO:

> Heritage is a broad concept and includes the natural as well as the cultural environment. It encompasses landscapes, historic places, sites and built environments, as well as biodiversity, collections, past and continuing cultural practices, knowledge and living experiences. It records and expresses the long processes of historic development, forming the essence of diverse national, regional, indigenous and local identities and is an integral part of modern life
>
> (ICOMOS, 2002, p. 4)

And going even further towards including both tangible and intangible, the Center for Heritage and Society at an academic institution characterizes heritage as the full range of our inherited traditions, monuments, objects and culture as well as the range of contemporary activities, meanings and behaviors that we draw from them (UMass Amherst, n.d.).

All of the three definitions given in the preceding paragraphs support an expansive concept of "heritage" that is society- and community-driven, that speaks not only to the past but to the present and future, that supports an understanding of heritage as the legacy of the past in the lived experience of today, that recognizes the passing of this legacy on to the future, and that is intimately connected to the ways in which a society understands itself.

Importantly, in these definitions, "heritage" manifests in no one specific form or format but encompasses the full range of human and societal expressions and activities whether they be material, non-material, or natural, including photographs, documents, books and manuscripts, as well as traditions, oral history, performing arts, social practices, traditional craftsmanship, representations, rituals, and knowledge and skills transmitted from generation to generation within a community. In addition, places and the environment are considered part of cultural heritage, joining community identity to the natural landscape.

Characteristics of Cultural Heritage

Cultural heritage as presented above has core elements that include specific contexts and environments, tangible and intangible expressions of societal and community values and evidence of these values over time. It exists simultaneously in the past and in the present, holds and creates memory, is both historical and dynamic, and tells and transmits the human narrative in multiple ways.

An example of the multiple facets of cultural heritage might be a Caribbean carnival parade with its tangible costumes, floats and traditional troupes, its intangible music and street performances, and its historical memory and community narrative. Like all parades, carnivals take place and are contextualized within specific landscapes. As annual events, they are transmitted through generations and, while the costumes and the themes change yearly, the overall ethos and motive of the event and its relationship to the community remain the same, and thus demonstrate the dynamic yet legacy nature of cultural heritage

Archival Heritage

"Nothing begins life in an archive" wrote David Lowenthal, "and few things remain there forever" (Lowenthal, 2007, p. 193). Sharing similar characteristics with cultural heritage, but evinced in more prescriptive and formalized ways, archival heritage perpetuates a multi-pronged human legacy, at the same time past, present, constantly evolving and, as Lowenthal suggests, selected over time. Manifest not only through records and collections, but also through the theory and practices that have managed and preserved these collections, archival heritage has evolved through centuries of record-making and keeping. In addition, beginning in the mid-20th century, an academic "archival turn" claimed "the archive" as fundamental to its humanistic studies and positioned it "as a metaphor for the accumulated and distributed knowledge of communities and subject disciplines" (Cunningham, 2017, p. 55). This perspective broadened the concept of that heritage, adding an academic reappropriation and re-imagining of the archival legacy that requires consideration in any archival heritage characterization.

Archival Theory

The Western codification of archival theory through the 19th and early 20th centuries drew on centuries of records protocols and distilled principles that have established a solid foundation for current practice. While the record itself, as both a concept and a representation, will be addressed in depth in the next chapter, the principles surrounding the record are basic to understanding it as heritage. Although these principles have been continually re-assessed and modified, they have retained their essential cores. Primary among these are the principles of provenance and its internal corollary, original order.

"The narrative of recordkeeping is about belonging – ownership of the records and of the truth that records memorialise. It is to be found in the attribution of what archivists call provenance" (Hurley, 2005, p. 112), writes Chris Hurley in his seminal essay introducing parallel provenance. Provenance is the foundational archival principle that dictates the arranging and describing of records in terms of their context of creation, that is, in terms of their creator or creators. It is the central organizing principle for archival collections at all levels. The creator may be an individual, a family, an institution, a government, a community, an event, or even a location. Provenance is essentially the circumstances that create and surround the record, which can also include the subjects of the record. Important corollaries to the principle of provenance are the ideas that records of different origins (provenances) be kept separate to preserve their context, and of original order wherein records are retained in the order in which they were received into the archive. In other words, archives are arranged, described and made accessible both in terms of the person(s), office or community that created or collected the records and in the order in which they were created or collected. *Respect des fonds*, under the umbrella of the principle of provenance, refers to maintaining records according to their origin and in the units in which they originally accumulated. These principles refer to preserving the organic nature of archival records as they flow from specific creators and/or circumstances and accrue in groups. Preserving this initial authenticating flow is essential in order for the records to be considered as evidence.

Developed in the 19th century by European archivists, provenance has undergone successive re-interpretations during the 20th and 21st centuries. Today provenance is understood, "not so much as a method for organizing records, but as an intellectual construct created through the archivists' analysis of the numerous relationships that exist between records, creators and functions" (Douglas, 2017, p. 33). The successive re-interpretations have moved provenance from the physical to the conceptual, and from individual creators and a single provenance towards concepts of social provenance, ethnic provenance and parallel or multiple provenances. Each step has contributed to the ambiguity of provenance but at the same time deepened and enriched archival heritage by expanding the meanings and values contained in records.

Social provenance points to the community rather than the individual as the creator(s) of the record so that the record must be understood within the context of community. As Tom Nesmith, who coined the phrase "societal provenance", explains, "Document creation, use and archiving have social origins. People make and archive records in social settings for social purposes. They do so with a concept of how their social setting works, where they fit into it, and might change it". Discussing the impacts that social circumstances can have, he proposes that archival materials be understood through a social lens and through the society or community that produces them, suggesting that social circumstances shape and dictate what and how information is recorded and described as well as who may access it. He sees society as "a kind of information gathering and processing phenomenon" (Nesmith, 2006, p. 352).

A year before Nesmith's exposition, Joel Wurl, then director of the Immigration Heritage Center in Minnesota, had proposed an ethnic provenance, which he described as a "social construct of group affiliation, not something inherently or genetically predetermined". Within that construct, ethnic groups "share a sense of common origin, embrace a distinctive history and destiny, and develop a sense of unique collective solidarity". He also theorized that ethnic identity was dynamic and changeable over time. Wurl was proposing ethnic provenance as an archival approach to managing the records of immigrant peoples and fully representing their experiences (Wurl, 2005, pp. 68–69).

With their emphasis on the cultural aspects of records creation, both societal and ethnic provenance offer possibilities for the accommodation of tangible and intangible record practices and expressions that move beyond the traditional textual. Emphasizing the context rather than the record brings cultural provenance to the fore as the primary descriptor. Chris Hurley reinforced this concept in introducing parallel or multiple provenance by which he meant "the ability to render alternative narratives about the same records" (Hurley, 2005, p. 124). Hurley writes

> parallel provenance is not about taking a different view of the same thing. It is about composing different things from the same particles – combining things in different ways to produce a variety of views of what they look like in the aggregate … It is not so much about identifying a different creator as recognizing manifold context
>
> (Hurley, 2005, p. 131)

This means that all the narratives involved in creating records need to be considered as the context of the records – the subjects, the communities, as well as the creators.

Original order refers to the internal arrangement of the records; it is an internal provenance in which the records exist within contextual relationships. Essentially, a group of records should be maintained in the order in which they were created by the individual, family, institution, or community, or in the order in which the archives received them. Knowing where and by whom, about whom and under what circumstances the records were created is critical to understanding what they are about. Locating them within specific contexts connects them to the actual events that they reflect. Keeping the records in the order in which they were created establishes their authenticity by presenting them within their original context of creation, purpose and use. Without external context connecting a group of records to a creator or to a society, and without an internal context that connects the records to one another, records become useless piles of paper or random collections of digital bits.

Although they are continually challenged and revised within the archival community, particularly in the digital age in which order may not be longitudinal but dispersed among data sets and must be reconstructed, provenance and original order can be considered as archival heritage. While each generation of archivists may bring new interpretations to provenance and may question or even reject original order, these two principles, with their roots in the context of creation, underpin the essence and purpose of archives – evidence, accountability and memory. Over centuries of archival activity, these principles have persisted as the unchanging inherited legacy supporting, sustaining and preserving the knowledge that is inherent in archival collections.

Collections

Archival heritage also refers to the contents of archival collections and the relationships of those collections to the creators of the records in the collections. The accumulated records of a government or a community over time are its archival heritage. National archives, community archives and a variety of knowledge institutions are dedicated to the preservation of that heritage. The attempted destruction of archives by aggressors in wars and the erasure of archives by governments attests to the significance, both symbolic and actual, of these heritage collections. Lowenthal notes that,

> Quests to magnify one's own heritage and to engross or suppress that of rivals are legion and unending. Romans strove to expunge Carthaginian memory, Nazis to eradicate that of Jews. From ancient Alexandria to modern Sarajevo, museums and libraries have been prime targets of enemy assault, with more lost to willful than to accidental incineration
>
> (Lowenthal, 2007, p. 200)

Questions of who owns that heritage invoke another archival principle, that of custody or ownership of records. In the 20th and 21st centuries, issues of custody and repatriation – two aspects of archival heritage arising from colonialism, wars and territorial claims – have attracted international attention. In 2016, the International Council on Archives established an Expert Group on Shared Archival Heritage "to provide a forum for the dissemination and discussion of issues related to the history and cultural heritage of more than one community, country or region where custody, ownership or access to archives is unclear or in dispute" (Banton, 2019, p. 19). This is only the most recent foray into the thorny issues of displaced archives and of claims that any country, nation or community is entitled to its own distinct archival heritage. These issues have emerged with increasing urgency in a post-colonial world, although the view of archives as valuable captured capital has been held for centuries.

The issue of ownership of archival heritage is as old as records themselves. In tracing its development in Europe, Ernst Posner observed in 1942 that, "A nation which is robbed of its archives loses more than heaps of dusty papers" and noted that the acquisition of archives by conquering and colonizing nations "was meant to deprive the subjugated countries of something more precious than paper–the silent witnesses of their individuality and their independence" (Posner, 1942, pp. 147–148). In 1977, UNESCO commissioned a report on archival claims. Its author, Charles Kecskeméti, quoted a summary of the views on the importance of archives of experts who met in 1976 who concluded that, "Archives are an essential part of the heritage of any national community. They not only document the historical, cultural and economic development of a country and provide a basis for a national identity they are also a basic source of evidence needed to assert the rights of individual citizens" (Kecskeméti, 1977, p. 7). Throughout the 20th century and into the 21st century, numerous nations have made efforts to reclaim their patrimony with very limited success. (Lowry, 2017). This aspect of archival heritage is on the one hand acknowledged as essential for the well-being of a community or a nation, but is on the other hand constantly at risk, not only from the actions of humans referred to above, but also from neglect, lack of care and, increasingly, lack of technological sustainability.

The Archival Turn

The archive as a focus of academic inquiry emerged in the late 20th century, partly in response to postmodernism and influenced by the writings of Jacques Derrida (1995). Known as the "archival turn", academic fascination with the archive has continued and grown stronger, so that it now appears to be firmly established as a central identifier and research focus of many disciplines in the humanities and social sciences. The archival turn differs significantly from the two aspects of archival heritage described above, aspects which are a part of archival praxis in which preservation and accessibility are central concerns of archivists managing collections of archives. The archival turn is an academic endeavor that has brought archival heritage to the fore as a critical metaphor for the knowledge that extends beyond traditional archives to encompass Derrida's "known and unknown archive" (Derrida, 1995, p. 36). To archival theory, we might add "archive" theory as a developing component of archival heritage.

What each academic discipline means by "the archive" or the "archival turn" may differ slightly, but sufficient commonalities suggest a general understanding that, "the archive" – in both digital and analog realms – is recognized as an essential knowledge space to be approached, constructed and even confronted in numerous ways and from many perspectives. Environmentalist and historian William Turkel expresses this broad understanding in his claim that, "Every place is an archive, one that bears material traces of the past in the very substance of the past" (Turkel, 2007, p. 66).

Knowledge spaces, sites of power, cultural anxiety, reading against the grain, disruption, post-colonialism are only some of the terms associated with the current archival turn. In order to understand the archival turn as heritage, it is necessary to go back to its roots in the early 19th century when historians, led by Leopold von Ranke, turned towards archival documentation as the essential evidence needed for historical truth and began to "equate professional historical studies with scholarship based on archival research" (Herman, 2013, p. 68). Previously, history had been struggling to become an independent discipline, and it was not until the late 17th and early 18th centuries that history became "increasingly accepted as independently valuable without the validation of the universal principles of philosophy or the coherence of rhetoric" (Eskildsen, 2013, p. 10). As in other academic scholarship of the time, the tools of the historian were empirical, relying on philosophical reconstructions, first-hand accounts, grand narratives, and the work of previous historians. Von Ranke and his followers focused on texts, primarily those found in archives. His "turn" included a belief in historical objectivity, historical truth and trustworthiness. Through the use of primary sources in the archives, "one could trust the work of one's fellow historians because one understood and shared their procedures of working and writing. Even historians who did not share Ranke's belief in historical objectivity described critical methods as such a guarantee" (Eskildsen, 2013, p. 19).

This first "turn" established a methodological terrain for the discipline of history that persists today. But, from the mid-20th century, a new kind of "archival turn" or "(re)turn" fostered a redefinition of the relationship of the archives to historical scholarship that not only questioned historical truth but also re-imagined historical sources. This archive expanded beyond the text to include memory, witnessing, materiality, performance and art – a broad and deep spectrum of "known and unknown".

This expansive view of the archive helped construct a conceptual and analytical space for discourse in a range of disciplines within the humanities and social sciences. It relocated the archive as a theoretical metaphorical space and potentially as many physical spaces. In this formulation, for example, a historian pursuing the archival silences of colonialism might interrogate "colonialism's archive", meaning all the relevant, existing, silenced and potential knowledge in a vast array of archival materials across a wide range of locations. "Colonialism's archive" is in no single place and is never completely knowable; rather it is an imaginary with no specific location but existing wherever the material might be – in traditional archives but also in the abstract and in the possible. The recovery of silenced voices, specifically those of the colonized, may not be attainable through conventional sources, but may, nonetheless, be imagined and reconstructed through such re-thinking of the archive.

Many disciplines in the social sciences and humanities have embraced the archive as a core knowledge site, and engaging and interrogating the archive has become a paramount academic activity. Whether the archive is considered in terms of film, photography, art, literature, history, anthropology, performance arts, or rhetoric, each discipline establishes and develops its own particular constructs and meanings. Each discipline sees the archive as an essential part of its heritage.

While each discipline may focus on its own formulations, there are commonalities, including the perception of the archive as the core but dispersed resource for specific disciplines. Feminist Kate Eichhorn writes that, "Since the 'archival turn' in the Humanities and Social sciences, it has been commonplace to understand the archive as something that exists well beyond the boundaries of the institutions that have historically authorized their existence" (Eichhorn, 2010, p. 623). Importantly, this archive is often digital, with the affordances of digitalization enabling the linking and data mining across complementary or even seemingly disparate and unrelated collections. In fact, one could say that these technological affordances are vital to the existence of the scholarly archive. In an example from the humanities, a forum of literary scholars critically examines the current path of literary criticism in terms of the archival turn, concluding that the archive was, "a way of guarding literary studies against accusations of interpretive triviality", and that its importance was in its function as evidence (Hyde, 2014, p. 157).

But, while converts to the archival turn in various disciplines have many commonalities and might also agree as to the increasing significance given to the archive as the means by which historical knowledge and remembrances are accumulated and recovered, they differ in their perceptions of exactly how the turn impacts their own particular knowledge spaces. A working artist sees her studio as her personal creative archive, recognizing that, "the studio as an archive is clearly a space of productive remembrance" (Sjöholm, 2014, p. 512). Anthropologists find that "the reflexive turn from the 1980s led scholars to question more explicitly the role of archives, just as they had become accustomed to questioning the contents of documents. They began to explore the implications of thinking of documents and the archives that held them as social artefacts" (Trundle, 2011, p. 408). Anthropologist David Scott considers the post-colonial archives in terms of both power dynamics and path to cumulative knowledge about any one topic or person. His definition of the archive accords very well with its cultural heritage implications: "An archive therefore is an implicit and constitutive part of the epistemic background of any knowledge, the dense network of allusions, events, concepts, images, stories, figures, personalities, that inhabit the sub-terrain of statements, animating them, giving them sense as well as force" (Scott, 2008, p. vii).

Considered as archival heritage, these different facets of the archive expand a way of imagining a heritage that acknowledges the potential existence of knowledge waiting to be uncovered. Archivists, themselves, who tend to emphasize praxis, have struggled to come to terms with the "archive", but, as Eric Ketelaar notes, "Archival turns and returns challenge archival practice and archival theory to understand and apply a multiform approach" (Ketelaar, 2017, p. 228). In a similar vein, Adrian Cunningham notes the expansive and inclusive perspective of the "archive" pointing out that, "This metaphorical view of archives may be extended to non-western societies and their oral traditions, where the storage, preservation, and transmission of cultural knowledge are achieved by a huge variety of means" (Cunningham, 2017, p. 55). The non-traditional records of this addition to archival heritage suggest ways to expand, extend and re-think the traditional archives by incorporating and presenting the texts of the unremembered, the forgotten and the marginalized. This expanded cultural archives encompasses monuments, quilts and tattoos. It references the records of small communities and the socially marginalized, as well the mainstream activites of the wider society; it identifies texts as expressions and signifiers such as dance, ritual and celebrations; it concerns itself with remembrance and collective identity.

Conclusion: Cultural Heritage/Archival Heritage – Points of Connection

Are archival heritage and cultural heritage one and the same, or, if not synonymous, are they closely related? Has the siloing and separating of each given rise to a false dichotomy that has created inflexible boundaries? While in Western tradition there may be a sharp division between the scribal and the oral, the written and the spoken, the fixed and the dynamic, in non-Western traditions the cultural is often archival and the archival is expressed through the cultural. For example, returning to our Carnival parade above, we are witnessing a cultural tradition but also the documenting of a community played out for us in visual and oral formats as the various troupes and floupes[1] depict both memories from the past and commentary on the present. Similarly, in societies throughout the world, traditional ceremonies recall and celebrate the past while updating the past into the present.

Characteristics of cultural heritage include a wide variety of objects, artifacts and sites, the tangible and the intangible. Their core focus is on context and they emphasize transmission, preservation, memory and community. Archival heritage through the centuries has focused on many of these same values, also with context at the center. Importantly it is moving towards acceptance of the idea that the tangible and the intangible can work in tandem, a core aspect of the cultural archives that will be further developed and expanded on in the following chapters.

Provenance as a value undergirding both cultural heritage and archival heritage serves as the first and most basic stepping stone towards the recognition of cultural expressions as archival. Modeling unity between archival traditions and cultural heritage requires an initial understanding of the basic concepts of both. To recognize why cultural expressions are also records requires moving into a deeper analysis of the record and its many manifestations. That basic archival unit, the record, will be analyzed in Chapter 2.

Note

1 Floupe is a portmanteau word for "float" plus "troupe" that performs in the Crucian Christmas Festival and St. Thomas/St. John Carnival parade.

References

Alivizatou, M. (2013). The paradoxes of intangible heritage. In M.L. Stefano, P. Davis & G. Corsane (Eds.) *Safeguarding intangible cultural heritage* (pp. 9–22). Boydell Press.

Banton, M. (2019). Shared archival heritage: An exploration of problems and solutions. Report of the EGSAH panel at the Yaoundé Conference, *Comma*, 2019(1), 19–28.

Bortolotto,C. (2007). From objects to processes: UNESCO's 'Intangible Cultural Heritage'. *Journal of Museum Ethnography*, 19(March), pp. 21–33.

Bouchenaki, M. (2003, October). The interdependency of the tangible and intangible cultural heritage, ICOMOS 14th General Assembly and Scientific Symposium, https://openarchive.icomos.org/id/eprint/468/1/2_-_Allocution_Bouchenaki.pdf

Butler, B. (2007). 'Taking on a Tradition': African heritage and the testimony of memory. In F. de Jong & M. Rowlands (Eds.) *Reclaiming heritage: Alternative imaginaries of memory in West Africa* (pp. 31–70). Routledge.

Carrie Hyde, C. & Rezek, J. (2014). Introduction; The aesthetics of archival evidence. *J19: The Journal of Nineteenth-Century Americanists,* 2(1), pp. 155–162.

Craith, M.N. (2008). Intangible cultural heritages: The challenges for Europe. *Anthropological Journal of European Cultures*, 17(1), pp. 54–73.

Cunningham, A. (2017). Archives as a place. In H. MacNeil & T. Eastwood (Eds.) *Currents of archival thinking* (2d. ed.) (pp. 53–79). Libraries Unlimited.

Derrida, J. (1995). Archives fever: A Freudian impression. *Diacritics*, 25(2), pp. 9–63.

Douglas, J. (2017). Origins and beyond. In H. MacNeil & T. Eastwood (Eds.) *Currents of archival thinking* (2nd. ed) (pp. 25–52). Libraries Unlimited.

Eichhorn, K. (2010). D.I.Y. collectors, archiving scholars, and activist librarians: Legitimizing feminist knowledge and cultural production since 1990. *Women's Studies,* 39(6), pp. 622–646.

Eskildsen, K.R. (2013). Inventing the archive: Testimony and virtue in modern historiography. *History of the Human Sciences,* 26(4), pp. 8–26.

Hall, S. (1999-2000). Whose heritage?: Un-settling 'The Heritage', re-imagining the post-Nation. *Third Text,* 49 (Winter), pp. 3–13.

Herman, P. (2013). The heroic study of records: The contested persona of the archival historian. *History of the Human Sciences,* 26(4), pp. 67–83.

Hurley, C. (2005). Parallel Provenance. *Archives and Manuscripts,* 33(1), pp. 110–145, 112.

ICOMOS (2002). The Charter. *ICOMOS International cultural tourism; Principles and guidelines for managing tourism at places of cultural and heritage significance*. International Council on Monuments and Sites ICOMOS International Cultural Tourism Committee.

Kecskeméti, C. (1977). *Archival claims: Preliminary study on the principles and criteria to be applied in negotiations.* UNESCO.

Ketelaar, E. (2017). Archival turns and returns; Studies of the archive. In A.J. Gilliland, S. McKemmish & A. Lau (Eds.) *Research in the archival multiverse* (pp. 228–268). Monash University.

Lowenthal, D. (2007). Archives heritage and history. In F.X. Blouin & W.G. Rosenberg (Eds.) *Archives, documentation, and institutions of social memory: Essays from the Sawyer Seminar* (pp. 193–206). University of Michigan Press.

Lowry, J. (Ed.) (2017). *Displaced archives.* Routledge.

Nesmith, T. (2006). The concept of societal provenance and records of nineteenth-century Aboriginal–European relations in Western Canada: Implications for archival theory and practice. *Archival Science,* 6, pp. 351–360.

Posner, E. (1942). Effects of Changes of Sovereignty on Archives. *American Archivist* 5(3) pp. 141–155.

Scott, D. (2008). Introduction: On the archaeologies of black memory. *Small Axe,* 12(2), pp. v–xvi.

Seitel, P. (2001). *Safeguarding traditional cultures: A global assessment*. Center for Folklife and Cultural Heritage, Smithsonian Institution. https://unesdoc.unesco.org/ark:/48223/pf0000132327

Sjöholm, J. (2014). The art studio as archive: Tracing the geography of artistic potentiality, progress and production. *Cultural Geographies,* 21(3), pp. 505–514.

Trundle, C. & Kaplonski, C. (2011). Tracing the political lives of archival documents. *History and Anthropology,* 22(4), pp. 407–414.

Turkel, W.J. (2007). *The archive of place: Unearthing the pasts of the Chilcotin Plateau.* UBC Press.

Umass Amherst Center for Heritage and Society (n.d.). What is Heritage? https://www.umass.edu/chs/about/whatisheritage.html

UNESCO (n.d.). *Intangible Cultural Heritage.* https://ich.unesco.org/en/lists

UNESCO (n.d.). *Memory of the World.* https://en.unesco.org/programme/mow

UNESCO (n.d.). UNESCO in Brief. https://www.unesco.org/en/brief

UNESCO (1954). *1954 Convention for the protection of cultural property in the event of armed conflict.* https://en.unesco.org/protecting-heritage/convention-and-protocols/1954-convention

UNESCO (1972). *Convention concerning the protection of the world cultural and natural heritage.* https://whc.unesco.org/en/conventiontext/

UNESCO (1989). *Recommendation on the safeguarding of traditional culture and folklore.* http://www.un-documents.net/folklore.htm

UNESCO (2002). *Universal declaration on cultural diversity: A vision, a conceptual platform, a pool of ideas for implementation, a new paradigm.* https://unesdoc.unesco.org/ark:/48223/pf0000127162

UNESCO (2003). *Database of national cultural heritage laws.* https://en.unesco.org/cultnatlaws.

UNESCO (2003). *Text of the convention of safeguarding intangible cultural heritage.* https://ich.unesco.org/en/convention

UNESCO (2005). *Convention on the protection and promotion of the diversity of cultural expressions.* https://unesdoc.unesco.org/ark:/48223/pf0000142919

UNESCO World Heritage Center (1992–2022). *World heritage list.* https://whc.unesco.org/en/list/

Wurl, J. (2005). Ethnicity as Provenance: In Search of Values and Principles for Documenting the Immigrant Experience. *Archival Issues,* 29(1), pp. 65–76.

2 The Anatomy of an Archival Record

Introduction

In 1994, archival theorist Terry Cook offered a succinct and compelling argument for record-making as a universal and enduring activity: "Behind the record always lies the need to record, to bear evidence, to hold and be held accountable, to create and maintain memory" (Cook, 1994, p. 302). That there is a connection between human activity, the recording of that activity and the imperative to leave a trace or representation of that activity, is an argument that is as apt and relevant today as it was when Cook wrote that sentence, perhaps even more so as digitization continues to complicate our notions of records. Wax tablets, papyrus, parchment, stone engravings, paper, film, computer bits, memory sticks, rock art, dance, songs, stories, celebrations, quilts and cloths are only some of the myriad configurations that testify to the human desire to "record, to bear evidence, to hold and be held accountable, to create and maintain memory". Oral, scribal, material, mnemonic, performative – all describe ways in which individuals, communities and nations choose to express, transmit and remember a narrative, fashion an identity, conduct business, control their environment, preserve their history and consolidate their memories. The reasons they choose to record and the manners in which they do so may be social, often necessary, frequently transactional, at times political and inevitably cultural.

The previous chapter described cultural heritage as encompassing a wide variety of tangible and intangible assets. From another perspective, the cultural record has been described by Ghanaian academic Edwina D. Ashie-Nikoi as "created both by individuals and by the collective". Quoting historian Stanley Chodorow, she portrays cultural records as

DOI: 10.4324/9781003091813-3

> The sum of the things we put away and drop on the floor as we, the whole society, go through life. It is the detritus of our ways of life and our ways of thinking, of our knowledge and beliefs, and of our superstitions and nightmares. None of these descriptive words outline the shape of something we can grasp, because the cultural record, which contains our cultural heritage, seems to incorporate the whole, unabbreviated body of evidence of everything we produce.
>
> (Ashie-Nikoi, 2021, p. 35)

Ashie-Nikoi notes that cultural records "are primarily created in the course of living, social interactions, relationships, and economic and political activity". Characterizing cultural records as a "'collective archive' of nations and societies" (p. 36). she hails records as helping to preserve the narratives of all peoples and essential to understanding the development of society.

For many, articulating and preserving narratives may be positive and empowering, a way of claiming identity and controlling one's environment; but for some, particularly minoritized or marginalized populations, expression has often been, and continues to be, a risky activity, suppressed through censorship, persecution, and even genocide. Yet, despite the dangers, people persist in finding many ways to keep their cultures and their stories alive, and these ways are often not in traditional record-making modes. A poignant example is the memory cloths created by the Voices of Women (Amazwi Abesifazane) project in South Africa, in which women shared their painful memories of apartheid by sewing and embroidering their stories onto fabrics. The cloths have now been collected into formal archives, "where the voices and texts of historically marginalized people can be incorporated into national projects of remembering and notions of belonging" (McEwan, 2003, p. 741).

In characterizing the making and keeping of records, it is important to keep in mind the negatives as well as the positives. The many manifestations of records have often served as elements of control and domination, as well as elements of freedom of expression. That records frequently held a menacing grip on the lives of ordinary people and that efforts were made to destroy records are threads that run throughout the history of recordkeeping. Historians writing about records in ancient Greece and in medieval Europe investigate the destruction of records, either as a planned amnesty to "wipe the slate clean" or as the result of civil unrest (Thomas, 1992). Similarly, French historian Henri-Jean Martin reminds us that "very early in history, writing served to remind people of the debts and obligations that they contracted with one another" (Martin, 1994, p. 74) and, more to the point in the recordkeeping context, that "writing was above all a means to domination and to the establishment of hierarchy, hence it was an expression of the ideology of a limited elite" (Martin, p. 27).

Yet, despite vastly different mechanisms of expression and the seemingly opposing reasons for recording expresssions, the universal and timeless need to do so suggests commonalities in both the mechanisms and the reasons. What is common and what is not common to different record productions? Can we, by analyzing the commonalities and differences, find the crucial points of intersection that expand what we think of as records, tie the act of recording, as well as the records themselves, to broader cultural expressions, and place what we think of as traditional records on an even plane and equal status with cultural expressions?

The range of cultural expressions is as wide and diverse as there are different communities and groupings of people. They may include monuments, oral histories, folklore, commemorations, landscapes, memorials, celebrations, memory texts, quilts and clothing. By connecting established record theories to these myriad expressions and thus demonstrating why and how these expressions are records, we extend the understanding of archival heritage and open up pathways for documenting cultural diversity. While the need to record may be a natural human impulse, that need arises in different contexts and with disparate and often contradictory objectives. This suggests a wide range of often competing values in the recording process, so that, to follow Cook's definition, for example, the mandate of creating and maintaining memory, may not be the same as the transactional requirements of holding and being held accountable. Bearing evidence may require different criteria in different cultures. But, while record-making and keeping may follow different paths, these paths intersect and inform one another as records become part of a continuing process whose contexts often realign over time. Accountability may produce and preserve evidence; what is evidence today may be a memory tomorrow.

Examining early recordkeeping practices, Geoffrey Yeo warns against assuming similarities across time: "Every society discovered a need for records at its own pace, and every society made, kept, and used records in its own way". But he also points out that, "while we should not assume that record-keeping behaviour in earlier times was always directly comparable to our own, we can identify some recurring features" (Yeo, 2021, pp. 187–188), and suggests that the challenges posed by records – protection, preservation and persistence over time – are common to all record-producing societies.

Mindful of Yeo's prescription and caution, this chapter examines the record – the fundamental unit of an archival collection – from the viewpoint of fluidity and change and as both a cultural and a transactional phenomenon. It proposes that, although records, record-making and recordkeeping have followed different paths, assumed different shapes at different historical moments and in different arenas, intrinsic values and similarities have persisted. The many and varied human reasons for record-making and keeping have not changed, even though the outward forms of the records made and kept, guided by community norms, customs and cultures, are liquid and mutable.

The Western model of relatively bounded, rule-driven records and archives developed through the 19th and 20th centuries emphasizes fixity and textuality, even in the digital realm. Such records are only one manifestation of what a record is or could be. Historically and globally, records, as representations and by-products of actions and transactions, are transmitted orally and materially through a wide range of forms and formats. Adding non-traditional forms and formats to the traditional panoply of textual records requires recognition of common attributes, functions and values as well as recognition of the diversity of formats that are today considered records and have been throughout the ages. Kimberly Anderson proposes re-assessment of the record, not by changing or re-inventing practice, but by broadening the concept of the record itself. She identifies the essential dilemma between the tangible and the intangible record:

> Physical capture is inherently framed within a context of linear time, and it fails to recognize recordkeeping forms that cannot be captured. Given these limitations, how is it possible to develop an inclusive archive? The solution can be found in the reconceptualization of the record. Rather than asking record-creators to change their recordkeeping practices or to submit to the possibly inappropriate static translation of dynamic lifeways, archivists can broaden their understanding of what constitutes a record—looking for and recognizing already existing records as they appear within different contexts.
>
> (Anderson, 2013, p. 363)

Roots of Record-making and Recordkeeping

The word "record" is derived from the Latin *recordare* meaning to remember, call to mind, think over, be mindful of (Record, 2021). The word "archives" is derived from the Latin *archivum*, from the Greek *arkheion*, initially used for the dwelling of an *archon*(a ruler or chief magistrate), in which important state documents were filed and interpreted (Derrida, 1995, p. 9). Although these may have been the roots of the words used today, they do not represent the first instances of record-making and archiving activities. Archivists in Australia, for example, note that,

> Recordkeeping traditions in Indigenous Australia are many, many thousands of years old and take many forms, including records embodied in people or contained within Country. They are "living archives" transmitted and accessed through storytelling and performance using speech, dance, art, music, and song … rock paintings and carvings; markings on message sticks.
>
> (McKemmish, 2020, p. 36)

Rock art, cave paintings, message sticks, petroglyphs and oral traditions make it clear that recording and transmitting information have always been basic human impulses. Paul Delsalle has written "Early humans, wherever located, all showed the same urge to make marks or leave foot or handprints in order to transmit information". He gives cave art and rock paintings as examples from South America, Africa, China and Australia dating back 40,000 years (Delsalle, 2017, p. 11).

Even rock art that is not as ancient as the examples Delsalle draws on is clearly identified as depicting a story, a message, or a narrative. As Connolley puts it:

> To encounter drawings and engravings on cave walls and stones, to observe sculpted appliqués and geometric symbols on pottery, and to determine from relative and absolute dating that they all belonged to a period over five centuries ago, is to be brought face to face with the ethnicity of an early people whose motifs have a story to tell.
>
> (Connolley, 2018, p. 651)

The San people are the oldest inhabitants of Southern Africa, where they have lived for at least 20,000 years. They are considered one of the world's most ancient cultures and are noted for their detailed cave paintings that tell stories of hunts, rituals and conflicts, as well as give an insight into their way of life. Many of their cave paintings are thousands of years old, but others, more recently, also depict the arrival of settlers in the 19th century (Vinnicombe, 2009).

Bullae, which are hollow clay balls containing other smaller clay tokens dating from around 7000 BCE, were used by the Sumerians to keep records of their agricultural goods and animals. They are thought to be the earliest examples of recordkeeping The tokens contained in the *bullae* were later impressed into easier-to-store clay tablets and, as Sumerian cuneiform developed around 3000 BCE, they too became obsolete.

While historians of archival origins identify clay tablets as early evidence of recordkeeping activities, they differ in their attitudes to whether ancient record functions are similar to modern ones. Ernst Posner asserted that basic record types were present in early civilizations, writing that, "in the great river cultures of the Nile and of the Euphrates and Tigris ... we find already those basic types of records that may be called constants in record creation, whatever the nature of governmental, religious and economic institutions (Posner, 2003, p. 3).

Subsequent authors also support the idea that fundamentals of recordkeeping were present in the earliest civilizations. Delsalle notes that "From the earliest times, archives have been part of the arsenal of government, helping to maintain control and authority ... Archives were considered to be among the most valuable, if not the most valuable, possessions of a conquered territory" (DelSalle, 2017, p. 226).

While recognizing that the "desires to identify the age of a discipline are surely legitimate", Delsalle, like Yeo, cautions against the danger of comparisons with contemporary practices, and of making historical equivalencies (p. 170). Anne Gilliland acknowledging that archeological findings from the Mesopotamian region suggest that recordkeeping "has been an integral component of human bureaucratic processes and business transactions in that part of the world" (Gilliland, 2017, pp. 35–36), also cautions against comparing or approximating the roles of archivists and recordkeepers today with those of ancient civilizations.

Many words have been spent on and a great deal of thought has been put into defining the record, which has given the record itself a long record of changing understandings of what it is and could be. Until recently, the cultural, non-textual records we are considering here have not figured prominently, if at all, in definitions. But perhaps there is a logical progression from Posner's assertion that records have been constants in serving institutions to an expansive understanding of records that encompasses a wide range of community expressions – from oral histories to monuments, from folklore to landscapes, from commemorations to quilts, from the tangible to the intangible. The genealogy of the record suggests that, far from the fixed definitions of the early 20th century, the record is a shape-shifter, a fluid and dynamic entity.

The development of formal record-making and keeping practices through the Greek and Roman eras suggests that as the Roman Empire expanded, the practices spread throughout the Mediterranean. DelSalle concludes that practices in the Roman empire likely intersected with those of the ancient Far East (p. 48). In China the writing of history began as an official function around the 15th century BCE; "The Ta-Shi or 'grand historian' was required to record the results of observations of natural phenomena and human events. He was astronomer, astrologer, historian and archivist – and in all these roles acted as advisor to the ruler" (p. 58).

Gilliland places the beginning of modern Western archival science around the 17th century when "the multi-ethnic empires in Western Europe began to break apart into nation states based around political, geographic or cultural identity" (Gilliland, 2017, p. 38). In the 18th and 19th centuries, theoretical archival treatises by French and German archivists were published, and by the late 18th and early 19th century, certain archival principles began to be codified, as noted in Chapter 1. It was not until 1898 that a comprehensive manual that articulated archival principles and gave practical rules on the care of archives was published. The *Manual for the Arrangement and Description of Archives*, by Dutch archivists S. Muller, J. A. Feith and R. Fruin (known among archivists as "The Dutch Manual"), had a major influence on international archival development (Cook, 1997, p. 21). It heavily influenced the work of Hilary Jenkinson, Assistant Deputy Keeper of Records in the British Public Record Office who, tasked with bringing order to the chaotic and voluminous records of World War I, codified a set of principles and practices that would govern the work of generations of archivists and recordkeepers for the following century. Most of the principles and practices laid down by Hilary Jenkinson were neither new nor universally accepted and challenges to them continue to reshape the archival profession today, but their initial formalization into a series of written precepts and processes established them as a base for Western archival thought.

Jenkinson's *A Manual of Archive Administration* (1922) was the first codification of archival principles in the English language. In the United States, Theodore Schellenberg's *Modern Archives: Principles and Techniques* (1954) was based on the practices at the United States National Archives. Previously developed principles such as provenance, original order and custody were not only re-affirmed but cast as immutable and gave rise to international standards and best practice. All three manuals greatly influenced archival development throughout the 20th century, not only in the West but also, owing to the reach of colonialism and Western influence, globally.

It is not the purpose of this chapter to detail a history of recordkeeping. Suffice it to note that, by the mid-20th century, the advent of digital records called for an archival reckoning and rethinking of the codifications and the processes and protocols that the three manuals had put in place. Championed by Gerald Ham and Terry Cook, the need for rethinking record-making and keeping in a digital world was presented as a stark necessity rather than a choice:

> At the heart of the new paradigm is a shift away from viewing records as static physical objects, and towards understanding them as dynamic virtual concepts; a shift away from looking at records as the passive products of human or administrative activity and towards considering records as active agents themselves in the formation of human and organizational memory; a shift equally away from seeing the context of records creation resting within stable hierarchical organizations to situating records within fluid horizontal networks of work-flow functionality.
>
> (Cook, 2001, p. 4)

As predicted by Ham, Cook and others, the digital environment of the 21st century has forced change in the ways in which records are created, organized and preserved. Digital affordances, as well as rebellion against prescriptive master narratives and concerns with social justice, have opened up new possibilities for recordkeeping and archiving. Today archivists are questioning the relevance of the three manuals cited above to contemporary social needs. In proposing a *(New) Manual of Archives Administration*, James Lowry and his colleagues write that, "today, recordkeeping takes place in an archival multiverse in which the rule-based, sector-wide manual is epistemologically inappropriate and always already obsolete" (Lowry, 2021, p. 3). Community archives and participatory archives have also taken up the call and are challenging earlier paradigms.

No challenges, however, have been greater than those posed by post-colonial nations and Indigenous peoples as they reclaim and assert their cultural identities in the face of a system that had ignored and disparaged their record-making traditions. Indigenous Australian archivist Shannon Faulkhead, for example, asserts that records are "any account, regardless of form, that preserves memory or knowledge of facts and events. A record can be a document, an individual's memory, an image, or a recording. It can also be an actual person, a community, or the land itself" (Faulkhead, 2010, p. 67). For Faulkhead and her community, records do not need to be fixed in time and space, or separated from the event of their creation.

The Chill of Colonialism

In the 21st century it is easy to forget that over the course of 400 years, from the 16th to the 20th centuries, a small group of European countries laid claim to large parts of the world. As detailed in Mandy Banton's guide to the records of the Colonial Office in the United Kingdom (Banton, 2015), the British Empire took pride of place in claiming the largest slice of the world, including at different times a vast array of colonies, protectorates, mandated territories and dominions on five continents, as well as many small islands. Other imperialist nations, such as France, Spain, Germany, Belgium, Denmark and the Netherlands also claimed their share. During the Age of Colonialism (better known as the Age of Discovery and the Age of Enlightenment in Western histories) rapacious nations engaged in a sustained global grab for territorial supremacy and economic exploitation, seizing and settling new lands that were often already occupied by Indigenous inhabitants.

In the general scramble for territory, many of these "possessions" suffered under a succession of "owners", but, regardless of who was in charge, records, recordkeeping and archives were central to the colonial enterprise. From the beginning, archives and records were deeply implicated in, in fact integral to, the colonization process. Maps defined boundaries and redrew territories; written laws, policies and regulations proclaimed from central offices controlled distant populations; records categorized people and property and tragically designated people as property. As Gilliland notes, "Vast bureaucracies were developed to administer colonies; manage the flow of information within colonial empires; support trade, slaving, and the extraction of other material assets; and enumerate, subjugate, 'civilise,' convert, enslave, transport, and even eradicate those who were colonised" (Gilliland, 2017, p. 38). Similarly, scholars of colonialism point out that, colonialism was archive-dependent from its earliest manifestations. Detailed recordkeeping and the knowledge created through records became a matter of life or death to the early European colonizers (Bailkin, 2015, p. 886). Historian Thomas Richards described the archive as "not a building, nor even a collection of texts, but the collectively imagined junction of all that was known or knowable … a virtual focal point for the heterogenous local knowledge of metropolis and empire" (Richards, 1993, p. 11).

Significantly, while colonial offices used records to administer their possessions, colonizers and settlers brought their own textual recordkeeping practices with them. Eurocentric recording and recordkeeping was imposed upon peoples with their own archiving traditions that were more oral and material than text-based. As the colonizers devalued the Indigenous inhabitants, the enslaved and indentured, they also devalued their cultural heritages, including their cultural expressions and recordkeeping traditions. Of the colonization of African societies, Ashie-Nikoi notes that the the colonizers "produced a mass of documentation related to the colonial project and not to the lives of the people. Indeed, European colonisers often suppressed any indication that Indigenous population had a history or culture of their own" (Ashie-Nikoi, 2021, p. 35).

European colonizers imposed their own recordkeeping practices upon populations that had previously flourished with their own different traditions, and the controlling negative aspects of records held sway. For those enslaved on the plantations of North America and the Caribbean, for example, "slave masters sought to assert their authority through relentless record keeping. And in the records they kept, the focus was not on their own actions but those of the enslaved on either the West Africa coast or in the field of enslavement" (Gikandi, 2015, p. 84). "The enslaved were not allowed to write or represent themselves … writing was a forbidden act" (p. 84). Despite harsh constraints, however, the enslaved found ways to communicate, perpetuate and pass on oral traditions that they brought with them from Africa as well as new practices that emerged through necessity. Tiya Miles narrates the story of Ashley's sack, a cotton sack packed by an enslaved mother for her nine-year-old daughter who was about to be sold; it was later embroidered with her story by Ashley's grand-daughter. Today through luck and the interventions of several generations, the sack is preserved and exhibited in the National Museum of African American History and Culture in Washington, DC. It is a testament to the persistence and creative energy of the need to record and to pass the record on. Miles identifies it as "an extraordinary artifact of the cultural and craft productions of African American women"; it is "more than an artifact. It is an archive of its own, a collection of disparate materials and messages. It is at once a container, carrier, textile, art piece and record of past events" (Miles, 2021, p. 6).

From the mid-20th century colonial powers retreated from most of the world and independent nations emerged in Africa, India, Asia, the Pacific and the Caribbean. Recapturing their traditions was one way in which these newly independent countries strove to re-assert their pre-colonial identities. In terms of their archives, however, the structures put in place by the colonizers persisted. In his memoir, Nicholas Dirks writes of his ethnographic research in southern India. He laments his inability to discover a pre-colonial archive in what he terms a 'modern archive', as opposed to the pre-modern inscriptions etched in stone or copper on temple walls dating to 600–1400 BCE: "much as I tried to escape the confines of the colonial archive, I kept coming up against its powerful tentacles and pervasive influence ... even after decolonization, the postcolonial nation had always to refer to the imperial power despite the reversal of the historical narrative" (Dirks, 2015, pp. 45–46). Thousands of miles to the south in a similar but familiar 21st-century lament, Jamaican archivist Stanley Griffin, tracing the Jamaican National Archives from its early colonial beginnings to the present day, deplores that "Jamaican archival institutions struggle to break from colonial patterns and archive 'records from below'"(Griffin & Timcke, 2022, p. 6). Researchers in Latin American archives concluded that "the reading of colonial ethnonyms and geographical imaginations from local archival collections has resulted in the subordination or complete silencing of Native pasts" (Erbig & Latini, 2019, p. 245).

The determination of formerly colonized nations and Indigenous peoples to reclaim and reassert their own records traditions has been a hallmark of archival effort in the 21st century. Protocols developed by Native American archivists and Indigenous Australians outline methodologies for the care and protection of Indigenous archival materials that are inclusive of cultural and ethical considerations (Aboriginal and Torres Strait Islander Network, 2012). In 2007, the Warumungu community in Australia in collaboration with researchers at Washington State University in the United States, developed Mukurtu, an open-source digital platform to "empower communities to manage, share, narrate, and exchange their digital heritage in culturally relevant and ethically-minded ways" (Center for Digital Scholarship and Curation, Washington State University, n.d.).

Finding the Record

Within this complex and contradictory history of record-making and keeping, how is it possible to find similarities and symbiosis in values, processes and structures between the records of the West and the records of the Rest (to rephrase Stuart Hall), between the textual and fixed and the less tangible and fluid, between the administrative, transactional archives and the archives of cultural expressions? Do these seemingly disparate entities have similar values, similar requirements and criteria that bind them together? The search for answers to these questions begins with the evolving definitions of archives and records.

Archives

Defining an archive and a record and differentiating between the two terms has exercised, challenged and confounded archivists since the Dutch Manual was published in 1898. This may be because, as Lemieux notes, "there is no one "true" conceptualization of the record, but rather many different conceptualizations of records arising from particular social contexts" (Lemieux, 2001, p. 82). To add to the confusion, the terms "archives" and "records" are often used interchangeably. The International Council on Archives (ICA) differentiates between the recordkeeper, who is responsible for the survival from creation of the record through to the archive stage, and the archivist, who tends to be responsible for the record at the point at which it becomes an archive (International Council on Archives, n.d., Who is …). Noting that different organizations and countries view and parse these two definitions differently, ICA observes that "both will have the same skills set and knowledge to ensure the physical survival and intellectual integrity of the archive". The ICA does not offer a definition of "record", but uses the term "records" within its definition of archives as:

> the documentary by-product of human activity retained for their long-term value. They are contemporary **records** created by individuals and organisations as they go about their business and therefore provide a direct window on past events. They can come in a wide range of formats including written, photographic, moving image, sound, digital and analogue.
>
> (International Council on Archives, n.d., What are …)

Differentiating between an archive and a record may be a matter of geography as well as semantics. Some countries, such as the United States and Australia, think of archives more in terms of historical materials and records in terms of current materials. Records, organized by records managers, are current and selected for deposit in an archives repository if they are deemed to have continuing value. In this way records become archives. The term "archives" may also be used for the building that houses the archives/records, a distinction that Schwartz and Cook parse:

> Archives–as institutions–wield power over the administrative, legal, and fiscal accountability of governments, corporations, and individuals, and engage in powerful public policy debates around the right to know, freedom of information, protection of privacy, copyright and intellectual property, and protocols for electronic commerce … Archives–as records–wield power over the shape and direction of historical scholarship, collective memory, and national identity, over how we know ourselves as individuals, groups, and societies.
>
> (Schwartz & Cook, 2002, p. 2)

Prior to the 20th century, archives were seen as administrative records generally in the purview of governments. Jenkinson's (1922) manual considered archives in terms of official government documents. Jenkinson argued that the job of the archivist was to ensure that these documents would serve as uncorrupted evidence of the actions of their creators, writing that archives are "documents which formed part of an official transaction and were preserved for official reference" (Jenkinson, 1922). In order to protect that uncorrupted evidence, he insisted that documents be retained in the archives exactly as they were received from the creator. He stipulated four criteria for determining that documents are archives: natural accumulation (meaning that the documents were a by-product of activity); authenticity; impartiality; and cohesion. Establishing the chain of custody, the path of the "document" from creation to acceptance into an archival repository, was essential to protecting the authenticity of records as evidence.

By the end of the 20th century, the definition of "archives" had expanded considerably. A 2005 publication of the Society of American Archivists offered a standard definition of archives as "materials created or received by a person, family, or organization, public or private, in the conduct of their affairs and preserved because of the enduring value contained in the information they contain or as evidence of the functions and responsibilities of their creator" (Pearce-Moses, 2005, p. 30). The Society's *Dictionary of Archives Terminology*, launched 16 years later in 2021, applies that definition to "archival record" and offers additional definitions for "archives" that recognize the collections maintained by community archives: "nonrecord material selected, preserved, managed, presented, and used in the same manner as archives" (Society of American Archivists, 2005-2022).

Perspectives on archives that are less official but increasingly relevant include a 1990 definition by Frederick Miller who asserts that the documents in archival collections relate to each other in ways that transcend the information in each document so that "the archival whole is greater than the sum of its parts; the relationships are as important as the particulars" (Miller, 1990, p. 20). Historian Steven Lubar offers a societally oriented view and points to archives as sites of cultural production that serve both to remember things after they happen but also to remember them as they happen (Lubar, 1999, p. 14).

Today then archives cover a spectrum; at one end they are a collection of materials collected and maintained according to a series of standards and at the other, they are living bodies of evidence and sites of continuing cultural production.

Records

There is more variety and nuance in the ways that records are characterized than archives are characterized. Yeo describes records as "persistent representations of activities, created by participants or observers or their authorized proxies" (Yeo, 2007, p. 343). Pearce-Moses defined a record in more traditional terms as "data or information that has been fixed on some medium … and that is used as an extension of human memory or to demonstrate accountability", but importantly noted that "the concept of record is ultimately independent of any specific carrier or format" (Pearce-Moses, 2005, pp. 326, 328). A record as "fixed", a record as a concept, and a record as a "persistent representation of activities" all suggest that the concept of record continues to evolve, particularly in terms of fixity. Electronic records have added to the difficulties. Amelia Acker suggests that "the project of defining a record should be abandoned in the age of networked records". She proposes a focus instead on "the ever-broadening layers of infrastructure and context through which digital records move" (Acker, 2017, p. 88). While these definitions propose that, conceptually, a record could be an activity that is not fixed, the question of fixity is ambiguous although archivists might generally agree that it must be fixed at some point and in some way in order to fulfill its archival mission.

No matter the terminology, there is general agreement that, first and foremost, a record serves as evidence of actions and/or transactions and, as Chris Hurley puts it, "denote a looser concept to do with remembering – anything from the terms of a formal contract to what information was communicated to whom in relation to some transaction, or just a note or log that something happened" (Chris Hurley, 2004).

Values

While the values of the record have long been debated within the archival community, most archivists generally agree with Cook, that evidence, accountability and memory are the fundamentals of a universally applicable framework for identifying what a record is and why it is being created. These values suggest that the impulse to record is an intrinsically human enterprise. Its many manifestations are only the outward representations of an activity that spans the centuries, expressing itself in pictograms as well as Instagrams, stone tablets as well as blogs. Bruce Dearstyne wrote in 1992 of records as

> extensions of the human memory, purposefully created to record information, document transactions, communicate thoughts, substantiate claims, advance explanations, offer justifications, and provide lasting evidence of events. Their creation results from a fundamental human need to create and store information, to retrieve and transmit it, and to establish tangible connections with the past. (Dearstyne, 1992, p. 1)

For Gilliland, 22 years later, "a record is always associated with some action, transaction, or event … ; and a record includes, at a minimum, a definable set of metadata that serves to provide contextual and other forms of evidence about that action, transaction, or event" (Gilliland, 2014, p. 176).

Other values are also identified with record-making and keeping. Yeo explains that his "persistent representation" is characterized by longevity and transmission: "It is a persistent representation because it has the capacity to remain available after the ending of the activity or event that it represents … Records may not last forever, but they outlive the immediate circumstances in which they were created" (Yeo, 2021, p. x).

Placing records in a more process-oriented context, Colwell emphasizes their social and cultural value, asserting that, "Records are products of social practices … In this sense records can be said to be practices, not the passive, objective artefacts that are by-products of business activity" (Colwell, 2020, pp.x,1). He identifies additional characteristics of recordness as completeness, reliability and integrity (p. 2).

In addition to these characteristics, essential defining qualities of recordness are structure, content and context. A record must have a form or format, it much be about something, and it must exist in circumstances that support its creation. Structure is generally identified as a record's physical characteristics as well as its internal organization.

Record structure makes the content intelligible. Content is the information in the record, what the record is about. Content functions as an extension of memory and is at the heart of the record. Both structure and content, organized and repeatable, support the idea of a record as a persistent representation. Context is the organizational and other circumstances surrounding the creation, accession, and even use of the material as well as its relationship to other materials.

These three elements of records–structure, content, and context–together with the values of memory, evidence and accountability and the elements of persistence, transmission and social context, suggest a possible framework for extending the definition of record to encompass a cultural archive. Sue McKemmish takes this further:

> What distinguishes the record, archive and archives from other forms of recorded information is not [just] that they have content, structure and content but that the evidence-related nature of their content … the specific documentary forms (structures) which they take and their particular contexts of creation, management and use have been preserved in ways which enable them to continue to function as evidence.
>
> (McKemmish, 2005, p. 15)

In other words, as Yeo suggests, it is the persistent representation of these elements that makes them records.

In summary, records, no matter what their format, may be characterized as particular types of entities that have certain commonalities. They may be identified as follows:

- The record is a persistent representation – "records represent those activities in a way that persists over time and that their creators had firsthand knowledge of the matters represented" (Yeo, 2021, p. 135).
- The record has structure, content and context – "Archival materials derive their value as evidence from a combination of three qualities: content, context and structure" (Millar, 2017, p. 11).
- The record is evidence.
- The record is authentic, reliable and complete.
- The record is not static but a dynamic process that may have multiple meanings over time –"The record is a repository of meanings some of which may be read in the record or inferred from the intertextuality that connects it to other documents; however, other meanings have to be deduced from the context

of record's or even archives' creation and use. I deliberately use the plural of 'meaning'; a record does not have only one meaning" (Ketelaar, 2012, p. 23).

Conclusion: Decolonizing the Record

Linda Tuhiwai Smith declares "reclaiming history [to be] a critical and essential aspect of decolonization". Reclaiming history, however, means contesting the accepted history of the colonizers; as Smith notes: "these contested accounts are stored within genealogies, within the landscape, within weavings and carvings, even within the personal names that people carried" (Smith, 2012, pp. 31, 34).

Oral traditions form complex knowledge systems that enable the reclaiming of history. Archeologists rethinking parallels between the oral traditions of different groups of Indigenous peoples on Vancouver Island point out that "Oral history can be a robust repository for intergenerational knowledge due to its embedded cross-linked narrative chronology and its use of geographically grounded place names and named actors" (McKechnie, 2015, p. 194). Anderson suggests that rather than attempting to translate non-fixed forms into fixed forms so that they can be considered as having recordness, "archivists should begin to recognize the forms of records specific to the community with which they wish to engage" (Anderson, 2013, p. 363). The assertions of these writers suggest that social, cultural and political justice demand yet another iteration of the record – one that can find a way to expand its framework to embrace the wide panoply of 'the need to record'. The continuing evolution of the record suggests that there is ample space for development and that the only real requirement for a record is that it meet the needs of the society that creates it.

Recognizing the elasticity of the record may be the next stepping stone toward unifying archival expressions in the cultural archives. Beginning with an analysis of orality and textuality, the following chapters explore different cultural expressions, including oral tradition, folktales, dance, and celebrations, all of which represent dynamic non-fixed records to determine whether they share the characteristics of records as they have been defined in this chapter.

References

Aboriginal and Torres Strait Islander Library, Information and Resource Network (2012). *Aboriginal and Torres Strait protocol for library, archives and information services.* https://atsilirn.aiatsis.gov.au/protocols.php

Acker, A. (2017). When is a record? A research framework for locating electronic records in infrastructure. In A.J. Gilliland, S. McKemmish & A. Lau (Eds.) *Research in the archival multiverse* (pp. 288–323). Monash University Publishing.

Anderson, K. (2013). The footprint and the stepping foot: Archival records, evidence, and time. *Archival Science,* 13, pp. 349–371.

Ashie-Nikoi, E.D. (2021). More than songs and stories: The nexus between cultural records and national development. *Information Development,* 37(1), pp. 32–44.

Bailkin, J. (2015). Where did the Empire go? Archives and decolonization in Britain. *American Historical Review,* 120(3), pp. 884–899.

Banton, M. (2015). *Administering the empire, 1801–1968: A guide to the records of the colonial office in the national archives of the UK* (2nd ed.). Institute of Historical Research, The National Archives.

Center for Digital Scholarship and Curation, Washington State University (n.d.). *Mukurtu, Our Mission,* https://mukurtu.org/about/.

Chris Hurley, C. (2004). What, if anything, is records management? [Conference session]. Records Management Association of Australasia 2004 Conference, Canberra, Australia. https://bridges.monash.edu/articles/conference_contribution/What_if_anything_is_records_management/4004529

Colwell, C.W. (2020). *Records are practices, not artefacts: An exploration of recordkeeping in the Australian Government in the age of digital transition and digital continuity* [Unpublished doctoral dissertation]. University of Technology Sydney.

Connolley, I.C. (2018). Jamaican Taino symbols: Implications for regional chiefdoms and their chronology. In J.A. Bastian, J.A. Aarons & S.H. Griffin (Eds.) *Decolonizing the Caribbean record: An archives reader* (pp. 651–672). Litwin Books.

Cook, T. (1994). Electronic records, paper minds: The revolution in information management and archives in the post-custodial and post-modernist era. *Archives and Manuscripts,* 22(2), pp. 300–328.

Cook, T. (1997). What is past is prologue: A history of archival ideas since 1898, and the future paradigm shift. *Archivaria*, 43, pp. 17–63.

Cook, T. (2001). Archival science and postmodernism: New formulations for old concepts. *Archival Science,* 1, pp. 3–24.

Dearstyne, B.W. (1992). *The archival enterprise: Modern archival principles, practices, and management techniques.* American Library Association.

Delsalle, Paul P. (2017). *A history of archival practice* (M. Procter, Trans.). Routledge (Original work published 1998 as *Une histoire de l'archivistique*).

Derrida, J. (1995). Archive fever: A Freudian impression. *Diacritics,* 25(2), pp. 9–63.

Dirks, N. (2015). *Autobiography of an Archive: A Scholar's Passage to India.* Columbia University Press.

Erbig, Jr. J.A. & Latini, S. (2019). Across archival limits: Colonial records, changing ethnonyms, and geographies of knowledge. *Ethnohistory,* 66(2), pp. 249–273.

Faulkhead, S. (2010). Connecting through records: Narratives of Koorie Victoria. *Archives and Manuscripts,* 37(2), pp. 60–88.

Gikandi, S. (2015). Rethinking the archive of enslavement. *Early American Literature,* 50(1), pp. 81–102.

Gilliland, A.J. (2014). *Conceptualizing 21st-century archives.* Society of American Archivists.

Gilliland, A.J. (2017). Archival and recordkeeping traditions in the multiverse and their importance for researching situations and situating research. In Gilliland, A.J., S. McKemmish & A. Lau (Eds.) (pp. 31–73) *Research in the Archival Multiverse.* Monash University Press.

Griffin, S.H. & Timcke, S. (2022). Re-framing archival thought in Jamaica and South Africa: Challenging racist structures, generating new narratives. *Archives and Records,* 43(1), pp. 1–17.

International Council on Archives (n.d.). What are archives? https://www.ica.org/en/what-archive

International Council on Archives (n.d.). *Who is an archivist?* https://www.ica.org/en/discover-archives-and-our-profession

Jenkinson, H. (1922). *A manual of archive administration including the problems of war archives and archive making*. Clarendon Press.

Ketelaar, E. (2012). Cultivating archives: meanings and identities. *Archival Science,* 12, pp. 19–23.

Lemieux, V. (2001). Let the ghosts speak: An empirical exploration of the 'Nature' of the record. *Archivaria,* 51, pp. 81–111.

Lowry, J., Kinsey, R.L., Lusty, A., Hyman, E., Heitjan, P., Rettie, A., & Goetz, K. (2021). No manuals: Archives administration 100 years after Jenkinson's manual. *Journal of Contemporary Archival Studies,* 8, pp. 1–17.

Martin, H.-J. (1994). *The history and power of writing* (L.G. Cochrane, Trans.). University of Chicago Press.

McEwan, C. (2003). Building a postcolonial archive: Gender, collective memory and citizenship in post-apartheid South Africa. *Journal of Southern African Studies*, 29(3), pp. 739–757.

McKechnie, I. (2015). Indigenous oral history and settlement archaeology in Barkley Sound, Western Vancouver Island. *BC Studies,* 87, pp. 193–228.

McKemmish, S. (2005). Traces: Document, record, archive, archives. In S. McKemmish, M. Piggot, B. Reed & F. Upward (Eds.) *Archives: Recordkeeping in society.* Centre for Information Studies, Charles Sturt University.

McKemmish, S., Bone, J., Evans, J., Golding, F., Lewis, A., Rolan, G., Thorpe, K., & Wilson, J. (2020). Decolonizing recordkeeping and archival praxis in childhood out-of-home care and Indigenous archival collections. *Archival Science,* 20, pp. 21–49.

Miles, T. (2021). *All that she carried: The journey of Ashley's Sack, a black family keepsake*. Random House.

Millar, L. (2017). *Archives: Principles and practices* (2nd ed.). Facet.

Miller, F.M. (1990). *Arranging and describing archives and manuscripts*. Society of American Archivists.

Pearce-Moses, R. (2005). *A glossary of archival and records terminology*. Society of American Archivists.
Posner, E. (2003). *Archives in the ancient world.* Society of American Archivists (Original work published 1972).
Richards, T. (1993). *The imperial archive: Knowledge and the fantasy of empire*. Verso.
Record (v) (2021). *Online dictionary of etymology*. https://www.etymonline.com/word/record
Schwartz, J.M. & Cook, T. (2002). Archives, records, and power: The making of modern memory. *Archival Science,* 2, pp. 1–19.
Smith, L.T. (2012). *Decolonizing methodologies: Research and Indigenous peoples* (2nd ed.). Zed Books.
Steven Lubar, S. (1999). Information culture and the archival record. *American Archivist,* 62(2), pp. 10–12.
Society of American Archivists (2005–2022). *Dictionary of archives terminology*. https://dictionary.archivists.org/index.html
Thomas, R. (1992). *Literacy and orality in ancient Greece*. Cambridge University Press.
Vinnicombe, P. (2009). People of the Eland: Rock paintings of the Drakensberg Bushmen as a reflection of their life and thought. Wits University Press.
Yeo, G. (2007). Concepts of record (1): Evidence, information, and persistent representations. *American Archivist,* 70(2), pp. 305–343.
Yeo, G. (2021). *Record-making and record-keeping in early societies*. Routledge

3 Oral Traditions and Memory Texts

Prologue

It's a hot afternoon in St Thomas in the US Virgin Islands and the umbrellas are up in the courtyard of the public library. A large group of children sits on folding chairs gathered around a father and son who are telling folktales. As the father relates the story of the Boar Hog and the Gold teeth, playing all the parts in the local dialect, the son strums on the ukelele and joins his father in singing the little verse that is a critical part of the story. That the son is a local politician, that the father is the patriarch of an old and well-known Virgin Islands family, and that the audience has heard this story many times before makes no difference to everyone's enjoyment and to the camaraderie between audience and narrators. In fact, both storytellers and audience are united in their appreciation of their own folk traditions. That the public library is a solid stone structure built by the Danish colonial masters in the 19th century as a stately home for a Danish family but for many decades has been a house of learning and knowledge for Virgin Islanders seems only fitting for a community that has come into its own. And that this building accommodates both the written history of the islands and its oral traditions suggests that both of these sources of knowledge exist in happy partnership.

The story of the Boar Hog wid Gol' Teeth goes like this:

> A young woman declares that she will only marry a man with a gold tooth. A boar hog passing her house by chance hears this and resolves to be that man. He visits a witch and asks her to turn him into a man with gold teeth. But since he was really a pig and might want to do piggish things like root in the mud, she also gave him a song to sing to turn himself into a pig again. The girl's younger brother found out about this song and exposes the boar hog on the

DOI: 10.4324/9781003091813-4

> wedding day by singing the song and turning the man back into a pig. And the moral of the story – "all that glitters is not gold".

The storyteller observes that,

> "long ago, the stories were told to educate the children, to learn about the history and values of the islands, and for amusement and entertainment. Today, even if the stories are not serving the same purpose, the children love to hear them, and enjoy them, but most importantly, they learn about their history and culture through them".[1]

As in many folktales, there is also a deeper cultural meaning. The chronicler of this folktale notes that "the performance-centered text of 'A Boar Hog Wid Gol' Teeth' is a popular Virgin Islands folkstory in which there are overtones of class conflict where the young girl would not be satisfied with any suitor other than one wearing golden teeth in his mouth". She makes a further cultural comment: "this tale was usually accompanied by the remark that 'a gentleman is a boarhog,' which seemed to show the underlying hostility felt by the peasantry for the upper classes who exploited them" (Hassell Habteyes, 1985, p. 108). In his *Dictionary of Caribbean English Usage*, Richard Allsopp defines "boar-hog" as "a male pig … a man of piggish behavior", noting its use in a number of Caribbean islands including the US Virgin Islands (Allsopp, 2003, p. 108). The terminology, the performance, the venue and the audience all contribute to this timeless and persistent cultural event which tells a story and carries a message.

Introduction

While "A Boar Hog Wid Gol' Teeth" might not be considered a record in the traditional Western sense, it fits well into a cultural lexicography of both the Virgin Islands and the Caribbean where this story is told along with many others across the islands, each having its own particular favorites but all fitting within a familiar narrative tradition. This folkstory also fits within the worldwide pantheon of folktales, which is only one of many oral traditions, which include a panoply of human communication, rituals, songs, genealogies and laws.

Jan Vansina defines oral tradition as,

> the respected lore of the past; it has a tradition, whether it purports to tell specifically what happened in the past (historical

> traditions) or merely to take delight in the performance of oral wisdom, wit, or beauty of the past … Thus religious hymns, proverbs, and animal stories are just as much oral tradition as are lists of kings or royal chronicles.
>
> (Vansina, 1971, p. 444)

But oral tradition is not only of the past; for many cultures, oral tradition encompasses the dynamic and ever-evolving expressions of the present as well. The orality of these expressions does not preclude their function as archival records; in fact, just the opposite. As formerly colonized and other marginalized peoples seek to assert their cultural identities by affirming, and in many instances re-establishing, their oral traditions, those who document society must increasingly acknowledge non-Western modes and forms of communicating, recording and preserving.

For example, in thinking about oral traditions as records in the context of the Indigenous peoples of Australia and South Africa, archivists in those nations have pointed out that "'the archive has become a liminal space in which received Eurocentric professional wisdoms are challenged, and in some instances turned inside out'. It is a space where 'letting oral voices loose … can empower Indigenous peoples to resist the Western modernist cultural hegemony'" (Cunningham & Wareham, 2011, p. 2).[2] On the other side of the globe, an archivist discussing the role of calypso on the Caribbean island of Antigua notes that "oral traditional forms offer more than a means of sharing historical knowledge. They are the methods through which information is recorded". He points out that oral traditions not only provide useful knowledge in terms of archival processes such as description and appraisal but also the oral and the written add value to one another, providing contextual details for the written text (Griffin, 2020, p. 1297). Similarly, Ashie-Nikoi points out that in an African context, cultural records are often created in formats not considered within Eurocentric paradigms, drawing attention specifically to oral traditions as a significant way in which "people and societies remember and memorialise folkways, communal knowledge, events and experiences" (Ashie-Nikoi, 2021, p. 35).

Paul Delsalle used the term "oral archives" in his *History of Archival Practice* to describe an oral document or testimony that has been written down. Describing oral traditions in West Africa, he asserts that oral archives encompass many categories of expressions, from proverbs to genealogies, stories and myths, legal issues and even poetry. Importantly he also notes that what is significant about oral archives is "not the absence of the physical document, but the primacy of memory as an information carrier". He credits *griots* as historians and storytellers, as keepers and guardians of this information for the community, and as highly respected specialists who form "a caste recognised as preserving the community's shared heritage and responsible too for the integrity and authenticity of the 'documents'" (Delsalle, 2017, p. 77).

But an oral culture is not the opposite of a written culture. In all societies, the written and the oral co-exist side by side, only differing by degree and type of use. Ashie-Nikoi observes that even where written records exist, the oral record is still a central repository of history, tradition and indigenous knowledge (Ashie-Nikoi, 2021, p. 35).

This chapter theorizes oral traditions as active living records and memory texts that, like written records, speak to the present as well as the past, very often in a presentness/pastness configuration that conflates the here and now with the there and then. Before the written came the oral; oral traditions are not single-faceted but run the gamut of human experience and human action – from the entertainment and lessons of the folktale to the origin stories of people; from herbal and medicinal lore to critical information for daily survival and protection; from land and property rights to juridical issues. Oral traditions reflect on the material as well as the verbal, on the tangible along with the intangible, as they are evinced through performance, folktales and folklore, myth, ritual and landscapes, all of which function as memory texts that support and carry these traditions.

Within the context of orality, this chapter investigates ways in which cultural expressions are also texts that are "read" and operate as historical records and as evidence of actual events. Using landscapes and memoryscapes as extended examples, it builds on the concept of "memory text" as a metaphor for considering oral traditions as documents, hypothesizing that the identification of "text" as an "oral archive" offers a familiar way to examine and compare the characteristics of oral expressions and narratives with the characteristics of written records and facilitates the testing of both.

The Oral and the Textual

In his book *Orality and Literacy*, Walter Ong addressed the dynamic and contextual nature of orality:

> The word, in its natural oral habitat is part of a real existential present. Spoken utterance is addressed by a real, living person to another real living person or real living persons, at a specific time

> in a real setting which includes always much more than mere words. *Spoken words are always modifications of a total situation which is more than verbal.*(emphasis mine). They never occur alone in a context simply of words.
>
> (Ong, 1996, p. 101)

Ong outlines the differences between the oral and the more passive written or textual, pointing out that, while writing is a singular activity because "words are alone in a text", sound and performance involve so much more than just words. At the same time, he also recognizes that it is difficult to conceive of a purely oral tradition because "writing makes 'words' appear similar to things because we think of words as the visible marks signaling words to decoders" (p. 101).

The written then is to some extent a signifier of the oral. It is in this sense that we might consider the oral as a text. Ong refers to the "text" of an oral utterance: "'text', from a root meaning 'to weave', is in absolute terms more compatible etymologically with oral utterance than is 'literature' which refers to letters etymologically of the alphabet" (p. 13). From Ong's perspective, the oral utterance is not only the forerunner of the written but is more complex, because, by its embodied performance, it includes a variety of other indicators that enhance and add depth and nuance to the utterance.

Although in its nuances of communication and transmission, the oral may be equal to or surpass the written, this is not generally recognized in many Western countries, particularly in matters of governance and law. Recognition of the validity and legality of the oral tradition as record has been a particularly contentious issue in matters relating to land claims. Archivist Tonia Sutherland offers an example in her discussion of "heir property" (land passed on orally to descendants without written wills). This practice, common among African American communities in the southern United States, has had disastrous consequences for landowners in these communities. Sutherland writes: "throughout the United States, but particularly in the Southeast and Hawai'i, heir property is commonly passed from generation to generation by verbal bequeath and without written legal paperwork", but this system breaks down because "verbal bequeaths, or oral wills, are not legally enforceable in the United States—in no small part because there is no system, through design or contrivance, for oral testimony, oral records, or oral documents in the US documentary universe" (Sutherland, 2020, pp. 242–243). She notes that other countries with strong oral traditions have attempted to recognize oral traditions around property as legitimate records and faults archivists in the United States for their reluctance to develop and codify practices that go beyond the records needs of the dominant society to support minoritized populations. Although some settler nations, such as Canada and Australia, recognize Indigenous land claims and evidence based on oral testimonies, the textual quality of the oral is not generally considered a part of the Western archival tradition.

The *Dictionary of Archives Terminology* defines "text" as encompassing all forms of writing, including printing, and typing, thus acknowledging that a text could be words carved on a tombstone as well as words in an electronic format. The dictionary also includes a definition for "oral history", but does not give one for "oral tradition" or "orality" – two concepts that have not been added to the Western archival lexicography. Definitions of "text" in general dictionaries of the English language also confine the word to the context of written materials.

In several academic disciplines, however, "text" is increasingly used as a metaphor to signify or describe the inscription of meaning onto something essentially non-textual, such as a landscape, a performance or an object. Disciplines such as anthropology, archeology, geography and the social sciences have appropriated and expanded notions of "text" beyond the written word to describe landscapes and other materialities that can be "read" over time. One might, for example, think of ice cores and tree rings as natural texts that scientists read for their information about climate changes and growth over decades and centuries. Additionally, technology and the many ways of configuring digital spaces have created new ways of combining, linking, and presenting a variety of formats and modes that, while dependent upon the word, also offer dimensions beyond the text, of which hypertext is only one example.

While some scholars may be primarily concerned with written texts, or with words on a page, others recognize texts in a wide variety of significations. Anthropologist William Hanks, for example, considers text against the background of a community. He locates text more in the social system in which the text is produced than in the actual structure of the discourse itself. He sees text within a social context, as a "communicative phenomenon" that includes "writing, oral performance, painting, music and other signifying practices" (Hanks, 1989, p. 96). Reflecting on the critical importance of both context and reception, he suggests that "textuality cannot be treated merely as a property of a limited array of symbolic objects but must be seen instead as an instrument, a product, and a mode of social action" (p. 103).

The communicative agency of oral text is also suggested by Mervyn Alleyne who asserts that oral tradition refers to texts produced and generally, but not always, transmitted orally. He places oral texts within the historical documentation of a society, as they

> either provide information about the particular genre at particular periods of history, and thus may be important for areas of social and cultural thematic history (songs, proverbs and so on); or they may also be sources of historical knowledge of the period when they were produced or of previous periods.
>
> (Alleyne, 1999, p. 36)

In other words, a "text" is a formulation or a phenomenon that can be "read" for its meaning. Not confined to words, it may be a landscape, a dance, a parade – any manifestation that involves human connection and interaction over time and conveys information. Similarly, historian Antoinette Burton, reminds us that "from the Rosetta stone to medieval tapestry to Victorian house museums to African body tattoos, scholars have been 'reading' historical evidence off of any number of different archival incarnations for centuries" (Burton, 2005, p. 3). She connects the text to an archive, opening the door to a wider consideration of what an archive might be.

Context is key to both recognizing and understanding a text. Hanks notes that "text … is … grounded in a locally defined social context, which functions as the source of information and author and reader draw on to flesh out the interpretation of the textual artifact" (Hanks, 1989, p. 106). Context then, similar to Ong's definition of the oral word, includes not only the creator but the receiver of the text, the conditions surrounding the text and, critically, the delivery or performance.

While there are many kinds of oral/material/performative texts, the reading/meaning of the text is dependent upon a number of factors, including how and by whom it is presented and received. Common to all differing interpretations of text is the idea that the legitimacy of an oral text rests within the society or community that creates it. The emphasis on context and on the relationship between the text and its creator aligns well with an archival record, for which establishing a "context of creation" is paramount to its authenticity; one definition of a record is what a community considers to be a record. Text as metaphor also suggests that a text is not static but is continually being reinterpreted by each generation that interacts with it. Similarly, archival records, although initially considered passive and fixed, as in the Jenkinsonian model, are today considered to be continually reinterpreted and repurposed. As Terry Cook points out, "evidence, testimony, and records are themselves social and political constructs, each subject to mediation, interpretation, bias, and power relationships" (Cook, 2003, p. 104).

Folktale as Text

To return to our folktale, how can oral traditions such as folktales also be considered as texts and, importantly, as archival texts? In the previous chapter, an archival record was characterized by persistence, process and evidence, and had three essential attributes – structure, content and context. Elinor Maze quotes William Schneider who echoes these attributes of oral expressions: "all stories [oral] contain at least three elements: text – what the story is about; texture – the way the story is told; context – the circumstances surrounding the telling … Taken together, the terms point to the hallmarks of oral tradition". Schneider foregrounds content, structure and context when he notes that an oral story is not only personal and creative but is also structured and "experienced by a group of people who share a basic understanding of the way stories are told and how to comprehend their meaning" (Mazé, 2007, p. 248).

Our folktale is also characterized by persistence; that is, while each performance of the same story may be unique and each telling differ in small ways, the central narrative is recognized and understood over time. According to Karin Barber,

> In oral traditions … it is clear that what happens in most oral performances is not pure instantaneity, pure evanescence, pure emergence and disappearance into the vanishing moment. The exact contrary is usually the case. There is a performance—but it is a performance *of* something. Something identifiable is understood to have preexisted the moment of utterance … It can be referred to.
>
> (Barber, 2005, pp. 265–266)

She also notes that placing the folktale within the wider backdrop of oral traditions gives it the flexibility and independence to adjust to the particular situation – which is what makes it an oral tradition. As Barber writes, "they are "traditions" because they are known to be shared and to have been handed down; they can be shared and handed down because they have been constituted precisely in order to be detachable from the immediate context and are capable of being transmitted in time and disseminated in space" (p. 266).

It is the essence of the folktale that the core story and the core message persist, while the actual performance will vary, depending upon the performer and the audience. In addition to the validity of content (text), structure (texture) and context, the folktale is also cultural evidence, as demonstrated by its multiple layers of meaning. If "A Boar Hog Wid Gol' Teeth" is also a tale of class difference and class domination, then this surely suggests attitudes towards historical social issues. If a gentleman is also defined as a boar hog then again this suggests class differences as well as gender differences. In the folktales of most countries, the essence of the tales is often an act of resistance, evidence of the attitudes of the dominated class towards those in authority. Anancy, the African trickster, and Br'er Rabbit, the wily survivor in the southern United States, are only two examples of a small weaker creature who outwits a larger dominant one in tales of defiance that have been told before and since the story of David and Goliath.

To speak of the legitimacy of the oral text or record as dependent upon the society that creates it acknowledges the centrality of collective/ community memory in determining meaning and passing that meaning on – a theme that will be developed in a later chapter. Sufficient for our purpose here is the acknowledgment and recognition that an oral, or non-written, text is the product of community, memory and tradition; in which a sense of past, present and future as existing together imbues a text with continuing relevance. Our folktale, for example, may speak to different generations with slightly different nuances. It could be about colonial domination, boorishness and greed, or it could be just a funny story about a pig, yet it retains a core message that speaks to whatever generation hears it. As Barber reminds us, the whole point of a tradition is its persistence as something agreed upon, shared and handed down by a community through generations.

Memory Texts as Archive

Memory text is a multifaceted term that both describes connections between people and events and how they are remembered and transmitted and describes the ways in which oral societies consider and locate their past as well as their present. A somewhat ambiguous term, "memory text" is also an apt term to bring oral traditions into the archival sphere.

Memory texts function as historical records and as the evidence of actual events. Echoing the connections between heritage and cultural memory claimed in UNESCO's Memory of the World program, Marita Sturken likewise suggests that "memory is often embodied in objects – memorials, texts, talismans, images". Recognizing that artifacts are often seen as prompting or triggering remembrance, she asserts that "they are often perceived actually to contain memory within them or indeed to be synonymous with memory" (Sturken, 1997, p. 19). Seen from this perspective, the object becomes a text, an artifact that carries a narrative.

V.Y. Mudimbe identified a memory text as "both a legend and a dream for political power. In effect, it links words and names to possessed things and spaces" (Mudimbe, 1991, p. 91). Within the context of variant versions of African histories, the oral narrative, existing in a space between history and legend, becomes a memory text. As an example, Mudimbe explored the origin myth of the Luba empire, a pre-colonial Central African state (1585–1889) that is now part of the Democratic Republic of the Congo. Analyzing the Luba empire narrative or genesis charter, he proposes considering this memory text,

> As a theoretical discourse which validates a human geography, its spatial configuration, and the competing traditions of its various inhabitants, simultaneously cementing them via this retelling of the genesis of the 'nation' and its social organizations. In effect, the charter does not recite exactly what happened but proposes an explanatory interpretation about how the country was occupied, a 'nation' organized, and a state ensured.
>
> (Mudimbe, 1991, p. 91)

Mudimbe speaks of the ambivalence of mythical history and historical myth which nonetheless contains an essence of the actual. The origin story of the Luba people, carried down through generations through oral tradition, is both myth and history – on the one hand, a memory and on the other a text.

This combination of myth, history and remembrance also resonates for Annette Kuhn who considers memory to be a process and a memory text, a performance in which acts of memory engage with a variety of objects. She envisions a memory text as a montage of "vignettes, anecdotes, fragments, 'snap-shots' and flashes that can generate a feeling of synchrony: remembered events seem to be outside any linear time frame or may refuse to be easily anchored to 'historical' time". In Kuhn's interpretation, a memory text is not linear, not fixed and may be composed of multiple disparate pieces which may all occur simultaneously (Kuhn, 2010, p. 299).

Memory texts are given an archival twist by Eric Ketelaar who places them within a social setting where, "Social sharing is mediated by cultural tools". He envisions these cultural tools as "texts" that may include a wide variety of forms, written, oral and material. He notes that, "the landscape or a building or a monument may serve as a memory text, while bodily texts are presented in commemorations, rituals and performances" (Ketelaar, 2005, p. 44). Ketelaar places memory texts in a broad societal context seeing them as interfaces between individuals and the past.

A memory text could also be seen as an object, narrative or place that evokes memory in an individual or a community and combines the real, the mythic and the remembered. It is a text that exists in the past and the present, as well as in the collective memory of a group or a community. While a past memory is evoked, it is acted on or reacted to in the present.

By considering oral traditions as memory texts, we create space for considering a wide and evolving variety of events and expressions as archival records that co-exist with and augment the written. In her analysis of the recordkeeping of the Australian Indigenous Koorie people, Shannon Faulkhead expresses this concept: "Oral tradition is a living tradition; it not only involves unchanging narratives, but also forgets other narratives and creates new ones. This process is undertaken to ensure the survival of the people and the land to which they belong". She sees oral and written records as a continuous interchange where knowledge "moves fluidly between the two forms, interacting, complementing and completing narratives" (Faulkhead, 2010, pp. 69, 65).

Reading the Text

Landscapes

Memory texts animate knowledge and oral tradition in many ways, both present and past. A memory text can be a series of photographs, a performance, a monument, a ritual and a place. Landscapes are compelling memory texts whose readings resonate within their communities as historian William Turkel notes, "deciphering the material evidence of human imprints on the earth – or 'reading the landscape' – is 'a humane art, unrestricted to any profession, unbounded by any field" (Turkel, 2007, p. xi). Caribbean archivist Stephen Butters has given an example; his account (Butters, 2022) is adapted in the following paragraph.

In the center of St Johns, the capital of Antigua sits the Antigua Recreation Ground (ARG), a large public space initially the site of a Whites-only cricket club in 1864 for British colonizers and surrounded by colonial offices, including the prison. Gradually taken over by Black West Indian cricket teams, it became the proving ground for premier West Indian cricketers and in 1981 was recognized as an international test cricketing venue by the International Cricket Council. It was the site of Antigua's Independence declaration and is today a multi-disciplinary cultural space where carnival activities, football, concerts, track and field activities, independence activities and parades are held. For the people of Antigua, this landscape functions as both text and context.

Butters notes that as the ARG changes its purpose and its use, it is a text continually rewritten and reread that functions within the historical backdrop of enslavement and colonialism and, latterly, independence. Both text and its context reflect and mirror the layered collective memory of the community as well as the actual history of this small country, a history of oppression, perseverance and victory that is expressed through the multiple generational uses of this cricket ground. As Butters puts it, "The landscape can be viewed as a text that is perpetually shaped and reshaped from the years of information gathered through personal, collective and historical memories" (Butters, 2022, p. 76). It becomes an archive of knowledge amassed and redefined over centuries and millennia, layered records of the relationship between the land and its occupiers.

Implicit in a memory text, as in an archival record, is that the meaning of the text is dependent upon interpreters. The layered records of the land send different messages to different communities of people over time. But in an environment often overwhelmed by dominant cultural narratives, absorbing the nuances of a landscape that embraces the histories and stories of all its varied inhabitants also offers opportunities to access minor narratives. For example, Clayton Fredericksen, interpreting a historical site relating to the Indigenous Tiwi community of Northern Australia, writes "Narratives relating to a place are linked in space to form a culturescape, a physical place composed of localities where the events of the remembered past took place" (Fredericksen, 2002, p. 299). He reflects on the context and the textual landscape of local knowledge, acknowledging "the legitimacy of community prerogative to nominate those parts of the physical and metaphysical past that are relevant, and to have the final say in how places and objects are managed (or if they are managed at all)" (p. 289). The text of the landscape and the interpretations of the text is specific to all its populations over time and all are implicit parts of the entire text.

Geographer Ellen Hostetter likewise observes that interpreting the text of the landscape requires consideration of all its elements. She considers these diverse elements such as structures, environment and people as forming repositories of information that can be retrieved and accessed. Similar to Ong's analysis that the spoken word includes so much more than the written, she asserts that the reading of place is very different from reading traditional media: "Reading place requires one to go there, to move around in it, using not just sight but all the senses. There is no standard way to read a place, no predetermined structure" (Hostetter, 2016, pp. 65–66).

Memoryscapes

In her study of memory techniques in oral cultures, Lynne Kelley connects physical spaces with memory; for Indigenous peoples, "embedding knowledge in sequences of places in the landscape or on small devices was the fundamental technique for elders who were totally dependent on their memories to store all knowledge of their cultures" (Kelley, 2016, p. 296). Taking her inspiration from the songlines of Indigenous Australians through which "by singing the landscape, they could navigate from one sacred location to the next, taking in waterholes, sheltering places and sources of food", she notes that "the sequence does not need to be memorized; the landscape itself fixes the order and acts as a constant reminder of the action which took place there" (pp. 13, 21).

In a related connection, Paul O'Connor cites an example of folklore and folk memory in an Irish village whose people hold a strong belief in the myths and rituals surrounding their particular landscape and continue to observe a variety of folk traditions. O'Connor observes that, "None of these tales is connected with a specific date in the past. Instead, they attach themselves to features of the landscape (hills, caves, lakes), personalities … and traditional observances … Place and custom therefore play a crucial role as vectors of memory (O'Connor, 2019, p. 5).

He draws comparisons between the role of archives and of place in preserving and maintaining history and claims that archives preserve historical records at the cost of "fossilising the past", while place "supports memory as a living tradition with which its recipients feel a sense of personal connection". Memory and place work together through their shared location. Through the processes of oral culture layers of memory are woven into a common narrative (p. 5).

The Oral as Evidence

Michael Clanchy has traced the gradual replacement of oral evidence by written evidence in England and in Western Europe through the dramatic example of Earl Warrenne, who in 13th-century England brandished his rusty sword as proof of land ownership. Using the hereditary sword rather than a written charter demonstrated the slow movement of evidence and proof from the oral to the scribal. Clanchy wrote, "Only gradually, as documents began to accumulate, did habits of consulting them and ultimately depending on them become established" (Clanchy, 1993, p. 34). He noted that "the growth of literacy did not occur in a cultural vacuum. It replaced non-literate ways which seemed equally natural to those who were accustomed to them" (p. 41), affirming the strong existence of an oral tradition in the midst of an evolving literate one.

Evidence is at the core of the archival mission; it is the essential rationale for the keeping of records. All archival processes, from custody to organization to preservation, are focused on the primary goal of assuring the integrity and authenticity of the evidence in the record. The record, as a fixed object, is proof of an action or a transaction. It is the concern with fixity of the record that complicates the notion of oral traditions as evidence and has largely contributed to the reluctance of archivists to recognize oral expressions as records.

Vansina asserts that the standard rules of evidence cannot apply to oral tradition because they "were developed for the study of written texts, and implicit in them is the condition that messages be stable and permanent, not fluid and evanescent as oral messages are" (Vansina, 1985, p. 147). He suggests that in the oral tradition, evidence lies in the continuous and communal chain of transmission over generations and where "the information coming from more people to more people has greater built-in redundancy than if it were to flow in one channel of communication" (p. 31). He points out that,

> The truly distinctive characteristic of oral tradition is its transmission by word of mouth over a period longer than the contemporary generation. This means that a tradition should be seen as a series of successive historical documents all lost except the last one and usually interpreted by every link in the chain of transmission (p. 29).

Vansina's delineation of oral evidence as chains of transmission and as continuity has been borne out through the decades of land claims by Indigenous peoples, primarily in Canada and Australia, whose claims rely heavily on oral tradition. In Canada, the passage of the *Constitution Act* in 1882 opened the door to recognition of First Nations' land claims, but it was not until 1997 that Canada's Chief Justice identified oral history as a source of legal and unique Aboriginal evidence. The specific requirements of that form of evidence were elaborated on in a 2001 case before the Supreme Court of Canada:

> A claimant must prove that a modern practice, custom or tradition has a reasonable degree of continuity with a practice, tradition or custom that was in existence prior to contact with the Europeans. The practice, tradition or custom must have been integral to the distinctive culture of the Aboriginal people in the sense that it distinguished or characterized their traditional culture and lay at the core of the Aboriginal people's identity.
>
> (Frogner, 2015, p. 146)

Similarly in Australia, a watershed case in 1992, *Mabo v Queensland No. 2*, reversed the concept of *terra nullius* (land that nobody owned)[3] applied to Australia in 1835 by the Governor of New South Wales, 65 years after James Cook claimed the eastern portion of the Australian continent for the British Crown so that the claims of Indigenous peoples could be recognized. In 1992 the Australian High Court "recognised that Indigenous peoples had a system of law and ownership of their lands before European colonisation and settlement" and found that "native title exists on land if a connection to the land and surrounding waters has been maintained from before the time Australia was annexed as part of the British Empire and that the land has not been alienated, or transferred legally to another person, corporation or other entity (Higgins, 2021, p. 726).

Conclusion

This chapter has explored the concept that the oral is also textual, that the written originates in the spoken, and that societies exploit both in different measures. If the oral is also a text, it follows that these texts are records with the potential to become archives. Recordness does not rely upon the written word; it is rather, as detailed in Chapter 2, a series of qualities, values and characteristics contained within the text, document or collection of documents. In addition, texts may assume a variety of forms and formats that speak to the culture and the identity of the communities that create and hold them. As DelSalle comments

> If it is now accepted, in a world of digital information, that archives need not necessarily have a material or tangible form, the relevance of discussing a similarly intangible method for preserving information is perhaps easier to appreciate. The term 'oral archives' sometimes sits uneasily with Western understanding of archives (the terms 'oral testimonies' or 'oral tradition' are often

> found as alternatives) yet the term 'oral document' is used in Africa itself for a document recording the text of a statement originally given orally.
>
> (Delsalle, 2017, p. 76)

The characteristics of both oral heritage and memory texts suggest that both of these intangible cultural expressions incorporate values and properties that align with those traditionally identified as being essential to archival records. As such, they form part of the cultural archives as do performances and performative expressions which will be addressed in the next chapter.

Notes

1 The storyteller is the late Ector Roebuck interviewed by Lois Hassell Habteyes for her PhD dissertation, *'Tell Me a Story about Long Time': A Study of the Folkstory Performance Tradition in the United States Virgin Islands.*

2 Verne Harris and Adrian Cunningham, quoted in Adrian Cunningham and Evelyn Wareham, "Introduction, Communities of memory: ideas from the islands on refiguring archival identities". Harris and Cunningham made these comments in a 2003 issue of *Comma.*

3 "Terra nullius", a land belonging to no-one, is a legal fiction created by British colonizers. On this flawed foundation, over a period of 200 years, settler invaders claimed the "uninhabited continent" for the British crown, extended British sovereignty over the Australian colonies and subsequently established the modern nation of Australia. Terra nullius was first overturned by the Australian courts in the Mabo land claim case in 1992.

References

Alleyne, M. (1999). Linguistics and the oral tradition. In B.W. Higman (Ed.) *General history of the Caribbean VI* (pp. 19–45). UNESCO Publishing.

Allsopp, R. (Ed.) (2003). *Dictionary of Caribbean English usage*. University of the West Indies Press.

Ashie-Nikoi, E.D. (2021). More than songs and stories: The nexus between cultural records and national development. *Information Development,* 37(1), pp. 32–44.

Barber, K. (2005). Text and performance in Africa. *Oral Tradition*, 20/2, pp. 264–277.

Burton, A. (2005). *Archive stories: Facts, fictions, and the writing of history*. Duke University Press.

Butters, S. (2022). Landscape as record: Archiving the Antigua Recreation Ground. In J. Aarons, J.A. Bastian & S.H. Griffin (Eds.) *Archiving Caribbean identity: Records, community and memory* (pp. 64–78). Routledge.

Clanchy, M.(1993). *From memory to written record: England 1066–1307*. (2nd ed.), Blackwell.

Cook, T. (2003). Evidence, memory, identity, and community: Four shifting archival paradigms. *Archival Science,* 13, pp. 95–120.

Cunningham, A. & Wareham, E. (2011). Introduction, communities of memory: ideas from the islands on refiguring archival identities. *Comma,* 1, pp. 1–27.

DelSalle, Paul P. (2017). *A history of archival practice* (M. Procter, Trans.). Routledge (Original work published 1998 as *Une histoire de l'archivistique*).

Faulkhead, S. (2010). Connecting through records: Narratives of Koorie Victoria. *Archives and Manuscripts,* 37(2), pp. 60–88.

Fredericksen, C. (2002). Caring for history: Tiwi and archaeological narratives of Fort Dundas/Punata, Melville Island, Australia. *World Archaeology,* 34(2), pp. 288–302.

Griffin, S. (2020). Where popular culture IS the archives: The archival significance of Antigua's calypso. *Journal of Popular Culture,* 53(6), pp. 1294–1315.

Hanks, W.F. (1989). Text and textuality. *Annual Review of Anthropology,* 18, pp. 95–127.

Hassell Habteyes, L. (1985). *'Tell Me a Story about Long Time': A study of the folkstory performance tradition in the United States Virgin Islands* (Unpublished doctoral dissertation). University of Illinois.

Higgins, N. (2021). Songlines and land claims: Space and place. *International Journal for the Semiotics of Law,* 34(3), pp. 723–741.

Hostetter, E. (2016). Reading place, reading landscape: A consideration of city as text and Geography. *Journal of the National Collegiate Honors Council,* 17(2), pp. 63–81.

Kelley, L. (2016). *The memory code: The traditional Aboriginal memory technique that unlocks the secrets of Stonehenge, Easter Island and ancient monuments the world over*. Allen and Unwin.

Ketelaar, E. (2005). Sharing: Collective memories in communities of records. *Archives and Manuscripts,* 33(1), pp. 44–61.

Kuhn, A. (2010). Memory texts and memory work: Performances of memory in and with visual media. *Memory Studies,* 3(4), pp. 298–313.

Mazé, E.A. (2007). The uneasy page: Transcribing and editing oral history. In T.L. Charlton, L.E. Myers & R. Sharpless (Eds.) *Handbook of oral history* (pp. 237–274). AltaMira Press.

Mudimbe, V.Y. (1991). *Parables and fables: Exegesis, textuality and politics in Central Africa*. University of Wisconsin Press.

Ong, W.J. (1996). *Orality and literacy: The technologizing of the word.* Routledge (Original work published 1982).

O'Connor, P. (2019). The unanchored past: Three modes of collective memory. *Memory Studies,* 15(4), pp. 634–649.

Raymond Frogner, R. (2015). 'Lord, save us from the et cetera of the notary': Archival appraisal, local custom, and colonial law. *Archivaria,* 79 (April), pp. 121–158.

Sturken, S. (1997). *Tangled memories: The Vietnam war, the AIDS epidemic and the politics of remembering*. University of California Press.

Sutherland, T. (2020). Where there's a will: On heir property, African American land stories, and the value of oral records in American archives. In J.A. Bastian & E. Yakel (Eds.) *Defining a discipline: Archival research and practice in the twenty-first century: Essays in honor of Richard Cox* (pp. 238–257). Society of American Archivists.

Turkel, W.J. (2007). *The archive of place: Unearthing the pasts of the Chilcotin Plateau*. UBC Press.

Vansina. J. (1971). Once upon a time: Oral traditions as history in Africa. *Daedalus,* 100(2), pp. 442–468.

Vansina, J. (1985). *Oral tradition as history*. University of Wisconsin Press

4 Carnival in the Archives: Performance as Record

Introduction

Whether as folk dance, religious festivals, formal dance theater, music, parades, or celebrations, performance is a powerful evoker and transmitter of cultural knowledge. Through their movements, gestures and actions, performers embody identity, tradition and memory. While each performance is unique and likely can never be exactly repeated it is this fleeting quality that adds to its legitimacy and cultural power.

Describing the Abbots Bromley Horn Dance, an ancient ritualized English folk dance performed annually in a small Staffordshire village, Theresa Jill Buckland suggests that it is the persistence and evanescence of this tradition that give it significance: "longevity of human memory is publicly enacted, demonstrating the ethereality of human existence and the continuity of human experience, as successive generations re-present the dancing" (Buckland, 2001, p. 1).

Observing dance theater in Peru, Diana Taylor sees the transience and embodiment of performance as an authentic and primary depicter of non-Western cultural knowledge. She draws a distinction between the scribal (the archives), and the performative (the repertoire), to explain how the repertoire of embodied memory – conveyed in gesture, movement, dance and music – offers alternative cultural perspectives to the written archives. Juxtaposing the dynamism of the repertoire with the static narrative of the archives, Taylor argues that repertoire has either been ignored or downgraded by Western cultures in favor of the textual. It is the repertoire, she claims, and not the archives, that expresses fluid and evolving knowledge in ways that text cannot capture. And she is concerned that innate scholarly bias towards the textual might predispose Western scholars to turn everything into a text or narrative, no matter the intangible nature of the subject. She suggests the term "performance studies" as a way of rethinking "the

DOI: 10.4324/9781003091813-5

repertoire of embodied practices as an important system of knowing and transmitting knowledge" (Taylor, 2003, p. 26).

Taylor's strictures about cultural biases also highlight questions inherent in envisioning cultural archives. Does placing cultural expressions as records within an archival frame run the risk of falling into a textual trap? Does claiming cultural heritage for the archives inevitably privilege the textual over the performative? Does the "reading" of oral expressions and cultural artifacts as "texts" discount not so subtly the essential qualities that characterize the oral and the performative? These concerns underline the cultural hazards of aligning "the Rest" with "the West" and many would agree that bringing the repertoire into the archives only reappropriates and diminishes it. But, despite the issues inherent in harmonizing the intangible and the tangible, alignment is essential if all cultural expressions – oral, textual or material – are to be weighted equally. Accomplishing that alignment while retaining the balance between these modes is the challenge. Taylor sees the repertoire and the archives in opposition, with the repertoire banished to the past, but she also concedes that they can work together, existing in a "constant state of interaction" as sources of knowledge and memory (Taylor, 2003, p. 21). It is in this constant state of interaction that we find the cultural archives.

This chapter explores performance as cultural record, addressing questions of cultural parity between the performative and the scribal by demonstrating that they can work in concert, augmenting as well as complementing one another. Taken together, the performative and the scribal offer the potential of a more comprehensive record, a multi-dimensional view depicting a social and cultural landscape holistically. That landscape is illustrated through a variety of communal examples of cultural performances, from formal dance to religious festivals, from parades to carnivals and where the audience and the creators are as much a part as the actors themselves.

Communities perform their cultures publicly in many of the ways already mentioned, but also in less obvious ways through foods, family traditions, speech and mannerisms. Not all performances may belong in the cultural archives, but for those that do, examining the tensions as well as the interactions between the physicality of the repertoire and the textuality of the archives is critical to incorporating them within that space.

Building upon Taylor's point that the archives and the repertoire may work together rather than in opposition, this chapter also suggests that these communal events are both self-documenting and documented externally: internally through their embodied performances, and externally through a variety of recording formats that may include text. The final section of this chapter models a performance within cultural archives through a multifaceted carnival celebration.

While some degree of cultural bias may be inevitable, it is by acknowledging the authority of both the repertoire and the archives that this bias can be ameliorated if not completely overcome. Only by considering both manifestations as two halves can an event be understood and described with an integrity that gives equal voice to both. The performative and the scribal can work together within a contextual interplay that reflect and record the communities that create them. In this listening for and assimilating all voices, the repertoire embodies the archives; the archives embrace the repertoire.

Dance

While Taylor imagines the repertoire and the archives as expressions interacting with one another, other scholars also suggest that they may work closely together. Jane Desmond explains performance as a cultural marker through visual literacy and codified representation, advocating for the study of dance as bodily "texts". Like Taylor, she points to the bias of the textual and encourages moving away from the verbal texts and object-based investigations that characterize European scholarship. Her theory that "dance is a performance of cultural identity" (Desmond, 1993–1994, p. 36) forms the basis for a study of concert dance in Barbados, in which dance practices act out the continuing debate between Afro-centric and Euro-centric ideologies and methodologies. Dance company director John Hunte, tracing the history of these two opposing concert dance traditions in Barbados through the Barbados Dance Theatre Company and the Yoruba Foundation, reflects on dance as both a documented and an internalized archives, concluding that "dance exposes national narratives around identity characteristics associated with race, class, and gendered identity" (Hunte, 2022, p. 94).

Tonia Sutherland illustrates the partnership between the archives and the repertoire through the work of American dancer and choreographer Katherine Dunham, creator of the Dunham Technique, who incorporated African and Caribbean motifs into the formal modern dance of her company. Sutherland points out that "the dances of the African diaspora were intended by Dunham to survive in the bodies of her dancers" (Sutherland, 2014, p. 25). She suggests that the Dunham Technique functions as an archival repository in which "each codified, culturally informed movement contributes to a gestural language that, with the proper visual literacy, can be read, understood and transmitted" (p. 153). The dancers themselves documented what could only be expressed by the dance itself.

Like the dance theater in Barbados, Dunham's choreographed dances are also part of formal documented archives. Physical repositories of Dunham's archives exist in several locations, including at the Library of Congress, which houses the Katherine Dunham Collection of field notes, choreography, photographs and film (Library of Congress, n.d.). The archives that live within the dancers themselves can be accessed partially through film, which offers at least one way into understanding visual performances. The written choreography and music existing alongside videos of performances may elucidate each, even though the evanescence of the performances will always remain elusive. Being able to view recordings of the performance at least allows for a more complete comprehension of Dunham, her method, her ethos and the cultural context of her dance.

Visual literacy also offers a way to recognize and identify the embodiments of dance. Operating through an analytical framework of form, context and content similar to that of an archival record, visual literacy requires a set of competencies for interpreting and evaluating visual media, such as analyzing the contextual, cultural, ethical, esthetic, intellectual and technical components of visual materials (Association of College and Research Libraries, 2011). While visual literacy skills have primarily been applied to photographs and art work, they could also be applied to performance, suggesting a strategy for decoding movement and gesture along with more conventional visual elements such as placement and design.

In a performance, structure may refer to choreography, configuration and design or organization of the work, content may include what the performance is about, its intellectual or emotional message, and even the dancers themselves. Context is the circumstances surrounding the performance, which may be its history, its traditions, composers, venue or audience. Whether an image is a photograph, a design, a painting, a website or a performance, visual literacy enables the interpretation and analysis of visual cues or codes embodied within that object or event.

Visual literacy is only one strategy for decoding and documenting dance performances. Arike Oke focuses on movement as the dominant form of expression. While she agrees that "the archives of dance ... is within the performers' bodies, within their lived experience", she also suggests that dance movements can be thought of as residues or traces of the culture that produced them (Oke, 2017, p. 201). She references the dance practice of "marking out" where dancers learning a new work code the movements into their bodies, and she proposes documenting dance through this encoded data. Oke argues that marking, a unique dance tool, "may one day be de-codable into non-performer readable and archival material" (Oke, 2017, p. 203), and advocates for bringing the embodied and the experiential together with more traditional documentary formats (p. 208).

Commemorations and Celebrations

While dance tends to be formalized and structured, other types of cultural performances, notably annual festivals, parades and celebrations, although they are not necessarily formal but are often highly structured, can also be seen as embodied performances, revealing narratives of cultural identity. Performance by individuals and by groups that present as a communal event is characteristic of many of these celebrations. Janet Ceja Alcalá describes a religious festival in Mexico where December 12 is a national holiday. On that day, towns and villages throughout the country celebrate Our Lady of Guadalupe with an annual fiesta. In the small town of La Plaza del Limón, where this holiday is celebrated in January, local videographers are commissioned to document the event so that it can be shared with the town's community and with family and friends in the diaspora. Ceja Alcalá describes the complex social structure of the Fiesta that involves the townspeople in nine different organizing committees, each of which leads and conducts one of the nine days of the novena. Each committee interprets and has responsibility for different aspects of the festival. In its final rendition, the Fiesta "is a performance on many levels. It is a religious performance in which the townspeople display their piety; a performance of the town's normative identities; and a performance that displays each committee's social status based on its members' ability to successfully curate the novena" (Ceja Alcalá, 2020, p. 226).

In the religious Fiesta in La Plaza del Limón, as in dance, the repertoire and the archives together complete the totality of an event that is both externally documented through the images captured on video and internally documented as its varied meanings are enacted by the participants and absorbed by the spectators. The records are the layers of individual and group performances as well as the videotapes of the performances.

Paul Connerton suggests that in a commemorative ceremony "a community is reminded of its identity as represented by and told in a master narrative ... a making sense of the past as a kind of collective autobiography ... Its master narrative is more than a story told and reflected on; it is a cult enacted" (Connerton, 1989, p. 70). Celebrations and parades often represent the prevailing narratives and values of a community, but they may also honor less dominant stories. They are documented in newspapers, flyers and posters, filmed and televised, and individually recorded on social media, but they are also embodied through the participants and spectators and through the overarching ethos that inspired the event; thus they constitute an aggregate of tangibles and intangibles.

Celebrations and parades reflect on and record the stories of their communities, both internally and externally, but they also function as demonstrations of political and social power. Studying parades in 19th-century Philadelphia, Susan Davis points to the many symbolic uses of parades, including self-promotion, patriotism, ritual and challenges to institutions and politics. She concludes that "at its heart, the repertoire of parades and ceremonies framed questions about power and legitimacy" (Davis, 1988, p. 159). This is demonstrated in two familiar United States examples:

- The National Independence Day Parade takes place annually on July the Fourth in Washington, DC, to celebrate the founding of the United States. The Parade's tradition dates back to the early 19th century. It is billed as "a major national event which seeks to draw the attention of Americans to the real meaning for the holiday" (National Independence Day Parade, n.d.). Independence Day is also celebrated at the National Archives by exhibits of its extensive materials related to founding documents. In small and large towns across the United States, it is traditionally celebrated by a parade that may involve town dignitaries, high school bands, community groups and often fireworks at the end of the day. But, as historian Roy Rosenzweig has pointed out in his study of leisure time among workers in Worcester, Massachusetts, there may by none of these celebratory activities as the day may be seen completely differently. He observes that the workers, primarily recent immigrants, rejected the parade but preferred to use the holiday for their own gatherings. His reviewer noted that his primary assumption was that the "Fourth of July celebration betrayed 'a release from, and an implicit rejection of, the discipline order, hierarchy, and sobriety of the workday and workplace and provided a vision of a less structured, less demanding, less constrained world'" (McArthur, 1985, p. 154).
- The Pride Parade, an international LGBTQ+ event celebrated annually in June, was initiated in 1970 in the United States to

> commemorate the 1969 Stonewall Riots in New York. Drawing millions of participants and spectators at parades worldwide, this event speaks to the power of protest, the desire for social justice and the affirmation of identity. The Pride Toronto website, for example, states as its goal: "We work to ensure equal rights and representation for every person of diverse sexual and gender identities. … [our] multifaceted membership is … united in its desire to be our true selves without fear" (Pride Toronto, n.d.). Pride Day activities are extensively archived both in LGBTQ+ archives and in more general archival collections. For example, the Boston Pride Collection in the History Project Archives in Boston, Massachusetts includes photographs, posters, and videos of the annual Boston Pride parade (The History Project, n.d.). The Pride Parade is a political as well as a performative event attended by large crowds of participants and spectators. It is a physical demonstration of power reinforcing the recognition that "as dramatic representations, parades and public ceremonies are political acts" (Davis, 1988, p. 5).

Annual events such as parades, commemorations and celebrations are complex performances. Part oral tradition, part history, part contemporary interpretation, part improvisation and part statement, annual celebrations and commemorations combine heritage, identity and prevailing attitudes. Often heavily contested and highly political, these events can also be protest movements, patriotic or even affirmational, signaling social acknowledgment. And they may change over time. Events that may have begun in protest and resistance, such as the Pride Parade, may grow in stature and community acceptance, while others, such as local Fourth of July parades, may become diffuse as different ethnic and class groups interpret the day to match their needs. As records of communities, performances are persistent and powerful markers that not only annually reinforce the identity of the parading body, but also chronicle social attitudes and social change within the community as a whole. While a parade will have its local organizing structures, the overall context is the community, and even the nation itself.

Performance and Provenance

Just as context is a critical element in oral traditions, context is similarly critical in understanding performances and celebrations. Recognizing the religious devotion of the residents of La Plaza del Limón, the

African roots of the Dunham Technique, the history of enslavement and colonialism in Barbados and collective struggles for recognition of the Pride Parade is essential for understanding these events and placing them within a background that connects them to the wider society.

It is through this lens of provenance, that celebrations, fiesta, parades and carnivals can be understood as archival. When the record/performance is placed within a particular societal context it acquires meaning and values that tell a story, document a history and serve as evidence of a particular narrative. The creator is not an individual but a community of individuals within a particular environment and cultural ethos. The provenance is often multi-layered, with a number of group and individual events existing within a larger event. The group or cohort that stages the event may be responding to a larger national or even international mandate, so the event must be understood through both the local community lens and the wider implications of the levels beyond the local community. Religion, patriotism, social justice and cultural identity are but a few of many motivations behind celebrations and commemorations. Connerton emphasizes the significance of the embodiment as opposed to the telling of the narrative: "What the telling of a myth does not do, and what the performance of a ritual essentially does do, is to specify the relationship that obtains between the performers of the ritual and what it is they are performing" (Connerton, 1989, p. 54). Furthermore, while these celebrations may become part of national narratives, their narratives are often contested within the very same space that created them.

Modeling Performance in the Archives: A Carnival Example

In performances, the participants, both individually and collectively, embody certain beliefs, histories and cultural identities. Nowhere is this better illustrated than in a Caribbean Carnival, where deeply felt traditions perpetuate and enforce cultural rituals that express the spirit of a community. Along with parades, commemorations and festivals, carnivals have long been considered indicators of public culture and as "key sites for illuminating issues of critical social, moral, and political importance" (Cohen, 1998, p. 190). It is in this sense that they are records of their communities. But do they also have a place in the cultural archives? The following example of carnival in the Caribbean suggests how the repertoire of carnival also becomes its archives.

Carnivals have an ancient and complex history. Initially a celebration before the fasting days of Lent, their origins have been traced back to a description of a festival in a Latin text from the early twelfth century, when "the pope and other Roman citizens watched a parade through the city, which was followed by the killing of steers and other animals" (Mauldin, 2004, p. 3). The practice of holding a festival, culminating in a parade before the religious observance of Lent spread throughout Europe in the following centuries. Contemporary European carnival traditions have been traced to the 15th century and are always associated with celebrations and extravagances immediately preceding Lent. The word carnival itself, from the Medieval Latin "carne vale" (meaning "flesh, farewell"), indicates that Carnival is the last opportunity to feast and otherwise cavort before pre-Easter fasting.

Scholars of carnival tend to cite the carnival theory propounded by Russian philosopher Mikhail Bakhtin who, in his study of the transition between the Middle Ages and the Renaissance in Europe, speaks of the disruption of the feudal order by carnival, which offered an alternative to officialdom "by suspending and/or inverting social hierarchies" (Taylor, 1995, p. 20). Carnival then represented an overturning of social norms – a resistance and a separation between serious and comic discourse and between the official culture of the ruling class and an unofficial folk culture. This sense of disruption and resistance and the overturning of social norms are clearly in evidence in Caribbean carnivals. Errol Hill, describing the early history of Carnival in post-emancipation Trinidad of the late 19th century, is quoted by Liverpool in his analysis of carnival as resistance, "Carnival had become a symbol of freedom for the broad mass of the population. … It had assumed a ritualistic significance, rooted in the experience of slavery" (Liverpool, 2001, p. 226).

The origins of carnival in the Caribbean are both European and African. It is claimed that French and Spanish settlers in the 17th and 18th centuries brought the idea of carnival to the Caribbean, but, at the same time, enslaved Africans shipped through the Middle Passage to the West Indies brought celebrations of their own, specifically masking and masquerading traditions. It is this mixture of traditions that inform festivals in the Caribbean today, where the phrase "Play Mas" is synonymous with masquerading and carnival. In Trinidad, for example, before emancipation in 1838, carnival celebrations were restricted to the upper classes, but after emancipation, the formerly enslaved embraced and transformed Carnival by incorporating cultural expressions brought from Africa (Ramsay, 2022).

Since the introduction of carnival-type celebrations, most island peoples in the Caribbean have adopted some form of the carnival tradition, calling it by a variety of names but making it a central feature of their cultural identity. Although the most famous carnival is held on the island of Trinidad, the celebration of carnival is also pivotal on many of the smaller islands in the Caribbean archipelago, where carnival-type festivities around Christmas and before Lent have been recorded since the 19th century. Today carnivals and similar festivals in the Caribbean are primarily secular events.

Hill suggested that the Carnival celebration is a recognition of, a reaction to, and a connecting link to a past collective history. It is an assertion of identity acted out by the participants themselves. The embodiment of Carnival is conveyed in the quintessential novel of carnival, *The Dragon Can't Dance,* whose protagonist, Aldrick, living in the ghetto in Port of Spain, Trinidad, creates his Dragon costume each year for the Carnival parade. The making of the dragon costume is described as an act of faith. It is by faith that he can build a dragon from scraps of cloth and tin. The costume is a message of beauty, threat and terror that he brings to the parade each year, but it is also a message by which he asserts his self before the world: "It was through it that he demanded that others *see* him, recognize his personhood, be warned of his dangerousness" (Lovelace, 1979, p. 36).

An annual Caribbean carnival is a multi-week event containing a variety of smaller events leading up to the culminating finale – the carnival parade. It is, however, an event that participants, designers, artists and musicians might prepare for year round. In addition to the elaborate preparations of costumes and floats, several pivotal public events precede the main event – the parade. While to the outside observer, carnival may seem to be chaotic, in reality, it is highly structured, with the prescribed events leading up to the parade carefully orchestrated by a carnival committee. With some variation from island to island, these events generally include a Carnival Queen contest, as well as musical contests, such as a Calypso King contest which features calypsonians from all round the Caribbean. Steel and brass bands also compete in separate events. From the various calypsos, a road march is selected by public acclamation which is often the central musical piece in J'ouvert as well as during the parade. J'ouvert, a traditional march or tramp through the streets from the early morning hours until daybreak, signals the beginning of the carnival parade. Food, drink and conviviality are prominent throughout and specifically featured through various events. In St Thomas, for example, a food fair and a week-long carnival village are opportunities for community gatherings. In the British Virgin Islands, a festival village serves the same purpose.

Calypso is a central feature of carnival and calypsonians vie for the title of Calypso King every year. Calypso, rooted in Kaiso from West Africa, is characterized by social commentary. It evolved in popular culture as a way of spreading both news and community information. During the coronavirus pandemic, for example, calypso provided a way of reaching the community to emphasize health and healthful practices.[1] As Griffin notes in his analysis of calypso in Antigua, "The calypsonian, like the griot and storyteller of other cultures, details the events, personalities, perspectives, and even attitudes that are prevalent in the society, especially at the time of the composition and performance of the calypso song" (Griffin, 2020, p. 1305).

The content of the parade might include commentary on history or current issues, or might just showcase intricate floats and beautiful costumes. Each troupe (or "band" in Trinidad) selects its own theme that might or might not be an interpretation of the overall theme for that year. While some troupes are "invitation only", others may focus on specific neighborhoods or may emphasize a particular age – clowns, for example, tend to be young, boisterous and often frightening. Masking, an important feature of carnivals, offers infinite possibilities for personal and social transformation. Certain traditional troupes appear every year, as do particular themes and particular performances, such as moko jumbies (stilt-walkers).

Caribbean carnival, primarily in Trinidad, has been well documented in print and visual media both within and beyond the Caribbean and extensively on the World Wide Web, but as one observer writes, "Caribbean Carnival is above all performative, and it cannot be fully understood through websites and print" (Farrar, 2019, p. 559). With its mix of oral traditions, physical performance and material artifacts, Carnival consists not only of many collections of records, both tangible and intangible, but conceptually as a persistent record whose long history can be traced through 19th-century newspaper accounts, government policies, novels, monographs and even commercial promotions. Its unique cultural contributions, such as the calypso and the steel band, also tell the story of Carnival. Just as Aldrick works each year to fashion the dragon costume that will proclaim his true identity, his effort blends seamlessly within a cultural tradition that recognizes his need and his right to do so. Even though carnival is performed differently on each island, its spirit is rooted in a common history of enslavement, colonialism and emerging nationhood; every year it reasserts the strength and resilience of Caribbean peoples.

Although each Caribbean island has a slightly different version of Carnival, the generic features described above, the overall context, structure and content, suggest how it might be considered as an archival record. A multifaceted event such as a carnival is tangible and intangible, oral, aural and scribal, historical, longitudinal and traditional. To view an event as a holistic record would involve recognizing each piece of the event using the tools of its repertoire as well as archival tools. Visual literacy can assist with understanding and analysis of the designs and colors of carnival costumes, floats and floupes, foodways in the village, and gestures of the performers. Movements, marked and encoded within the performers, who have known the rhythms of carnival since childhood, can be transcribed and interpreted. Archival values such as provenance place carnival within its local, national, regional and historical contexts. Original order presents the structure and organization, creating a hierarchy of events, each within an internal provenance that binds them together. Combining these components with visual and aural performances captured in photographs, film, video, sound and audience observations presents a complex narrative – a picture of carnival in all its components.

Elsewhere, I have suggested considering the parade as the central event, while the troupes, audience, presentations, themes, costumes, music and other elements might be so many spokes in a collection wheel, extending out into myriad small record series that together capture a holistic sense of carnival within the provenance of the community and the wider Caribbean region (Bastian, 2009). But there are multiple ways that the repertoire can enter the cultural archives using the tools of both.

Conclusion

"Ceremonies and rituals are human-made things. They must be studied in the time and space in which they are created" (Davis, 1988, p. 12). Representing performance in the cultural archives has limits and raises several questions. Can the archives identify, represent and preserve a dynamic event without changing the nature of that event? Can the intangible be made tangible without destroying its transitory nature and thereby its integrity? Attempting complete representation might be beside the point and may not lie in learning new techniques or methods unfamiliar to archivists; it may rather lie in the archivist's own acceptance of cultural performances as records. Recognizing and acknowledging the limitations is part of the process of documenting the repertoire. Historian Richard Cándida Smith describes this problem in the context of recording oral histories and the impossibility of capturing all the gestures and emotions that are inseparable elements of those encounters:

> Yet there is a conundrum that every interpreter of oral sources in the arts faces sooner or later. Visual and performing artists work in expressive forms and media that resist language. Interviews

> involve a translation from one level of experience to another … the need to throw immediate sensual experience off into words underscores the ambiguous if necessary relation of word, gesture and object in the consolidation of experience and memory.
>
> (Cándida Smith, 2002, p. 2)

A core aspect of a performance is the mutability and dynamism of the cultural event itself. No single video of a parade, no recording of one set of dance movements, no website of a carnival recording of one collection of songs completely documents any cultural event. A cultural expression has no end; it is always becoming something else. This evolutionary process of a cultural event means that documenting it is also a continuing and organic process. Nevertheless, while the archival record can never truly be the whole record, it can at least provide a sense of the whole.

The tangible and intangible nature of performance combines both written and embodied documentation working in tandem and demonstrating archival qualities and values. This fusion of the archives and the repertoire, the scribal and the perfomative, offers opportunities for positioning performance and performative expressions as cultural records and essential components of cultural archives. The next chapter continues to emphasize the unity of the tangible and the intangible as it considers the place of memory and community in the cultural archives.

Note

1 Leroy "Georgie" Straker's "De Corona Virus" video from Barbados is an example of such messaging: https://www.youtube.com/watch?v=50p3139Zpcw

References

Association of College and Research Libraries (2011). *ACRL visual literacy competency standards for higher education.* https://www.ala.org/acrl/standards/visualliteracy

Bastian, J.A. (2009). 'Play Mas': Carnival in the archives and the archives in carnival: Records and community identity in the US Virgin Islands. *Archival Science,* 9, pp. 113–125.

Buckland, T.J. (2001). Dance, authenticity and cultural memory: The politics of embodiment. *Yearbook for Traditional Music*, p. 33.

Ceja Alcalá, J. (2020). Fiesta videos: Living and producing social memory of El Rancho. In J.A. Bastian & E. Yakel (Eds.) *Defining a discipline: Archival research and practice in the twenty-first century: Essays in Honor of Richard Cox* (pp. 218–237). Society of American Archivists.

Cohen, C.B. (1998). This is de test: Festival and the cultural politics of nation building in the British Virgin Islands. *American Ethnologist,* 25(2), pp. 189–214.

Connerton, P. (1989). *How societies remember*. Cambridge University Press.

Cándida Smith, R. (2002). *Art and the performance of memory: Sounds and gestures of recollection*. Routledge.

Davis, S. 1988). *Parades and power: Street theatre in nineteenth-century Philadelphia*. University of California Press.

Desmond, J.C. (1993–1994). Embodying difference: Issues in dance and cultural studies. *Cultural Critique*, 26 (Winter), pp. 33–63.

Farrar, M. (2019). The Caribbean Carnival: Yearning for Freedom. *Caribbean Quarterly,* 65(4), pp. 553–574.

Griffin, S. (2020). Where popular culture IS the archives: The archival significance of Antigua's calypso. *Journal of Popular Culture,* 53(6), pp. 1294–1315.

Hunte, J. (2022). Concert dance in Barbados as archive: Dancing the national narratives. In J.A. Aarons, J.A. Bastian & S.H. Griffin (Eds.) *Archiving Caribbean identity: Records, Community and Memory* (pp. 65–78). Routledge.

Library of Congress (n.d.). *Selections from the Katherine Dunham collection, About this collection.* https://www.loc.gov/collections/katherine-dunham/about-this-collection/

Liverpool, H. (2001). *Rituals of power and rebellion: The carnival tradition in Trinidad & Tobago, 1763–1962*. Research Associates School Times Publications.

Lovelace, E. (1979). *The dragon can't dance*. Persea Books.

Mauldin, B. (2004). Introduction, carnival in Europe and the Americas. In B. Maudlin (Ed.) *Carnaval!* (pp. 3–18). University of Washington Press.

McArthur, B. (1985). Review of eight hours for what we will. *Journal of Interdisciplinary History,* 16(1), pp. 154–155.

National Independence Day Parade (n.d.). About the parade. https://july4thparade.com/about/

Oke, A. (2017). Keeping time in dance archives: Moving towards the phenomenological archive space. *Archives and Records,* 38(2), pp. 197–211.

Pride Toronto (n.d.). https://www.pridetoronto.com/

Ramsay, A. (2022). Crop over and carnival in archives of Barbados and Trinidad and Tobago. In J.A. Aarons, J.A. Bastian & S.H. Griffin (Eds.) *Archiving Caribbean identity: Records, community and memory* (pp. 199–212). Routledge.

Sutherland, T. (2014). *Restaging the record: The role of contemporary archives in safeguarding and preserving performance as intangible cultural heritage.* (Unpublished doctoral dissertation). University of Pittsburgh.

Taylor, B. (1995). *Bakhtin, carnival and comic theory* (Unpublished doctoral dissertation). University of Nottingham.

Taylor, D. (2003). *The archives and the repertoire: Performing cultural memory in the Americas.* Duke University Press.

The History Project (n.d.). Boston Pride Collection. https://historyproject.omeka.net/collections/show/40

5 Memory, Community and Records

Introduction

There is a carpet of sand on the floor of my St. Thomas synagogue. Its origins are mysterious, but legend has it that the original nine Sephardic families who founded the congregation of Blessing, Peace and Loving Kindness in the 1790s were honoring the memories of their ancestors, Portuguese and Spanish Jews, who, during the inquisition of the 1490s, put sand on the floors of their places of worship to muffle the sounds of prayer. While few descendants of those Sephardic families populate the synagogue today, the weight of the sand and its cultural memory remains, linking the current Ashkenazi community to the generations before, just as it linked those earlier communities to their enforced exodus from Europe.

The sand is mentioned in the US National Archives description of the Synagogue building for the Synagogue's successful nomination to the US National Register of Historic Places: "In accordance with local Sephardic Jewish tradition, the central floor area and the raised platforms of the congregation are covered with about an inch of sand" (National Archives Catalog, 1997). Sand is not mentioned in the short descriptions in the few archival collections in other repositories, yet the Synagogue website declares "The most commented upon and asked about feature of our synagogue, of course, is the sand on the floor … The sand on our floor is a tribute and a symbol, a historical memory of that survival strategy" (Hebrew Congregation of St. Thomas, n.d.). Just as a mortar of sand, lime and molasses binds together the rubble walls of the Synagogue, so too does the sand on the floor bind the community to its history and to its two sister Caribbean synagogues with similar floors and similar Sephardic roots. The sand stands as a potent cultural artifact and ever-present memory for their congregations.

DOI: 10.4324/9781003091813-6

Despite the omission of any mention of sand in official archives, can we consider the cultural memory of the sand as a record of this St. Thomas congregation and community? Do memory and the touchstones of memory have a place within our cultural archives? In this chapter, I present some of the theories that have developed around memory in the 20th century in order to explore the relationships between communities, records and memory – cultural, collective and archival – and to center memory as a legitimate correlative and claimant to the category of "record". Acknowledging that communities not only create their own memories but also determine what is to be forgotten, I consider the nature of communities and community archives and how these communities of records and memory inform the cultural archives. And since memory is both fluid and ongoing, I explore continuing developing relationships between memory and archives in the digital arena.

Collective Memory

Memory's status as a legitimate area of evidence has been growing since the mid-20th century. Today memory occupies a central position in academic scholarship, although it does so more ambiguously in the archival world. In the early 20th century, Maurice Halbwachs, considered the father of collective memory, moved memory out of national and psychological spheres and into social ones. His fundamental insight that not only do we see the past through the lens of the present, but that each lens is that of a group rather than an individual, positioned memory as both a socially constructed and a collective phenomenon. Halbwachs proposed that, "while the collective memory endures and draws strength from its base in a coherent body of people, it is individuals as group members who remember"; he concluded that "every collective memory requires the support of a group delimited in time and space" (Halbwachs, 1992, p. 22). From Halbwachs' perspective, collective memory is shaped by the specific nature of a group and its collective experience and, in turn, the particular nature of a group's experience creates a shared memory and identity. As a result, every group has its own collective memory – one that differs from the collective memories of other groups (Russell, 2006).

Memory studies in the late 19th and early 20th centuries focused on memory in the formation of national identities. Halbwachs' recognition that collective memory is a social construct and that individuals view the past in the present through multiple frameworks became the foundation for modern collective memory studies. Although he wrote his first work on collective memory in the 1920s, his concept of memory as a group framework and a lens through which we view the world may now be more relevant than ever in the current global climate of mass migration and struggles for social justice.

Despite Halbwachs' early intervention, it was not until the 1970s that the so-called "memory boom" exploded and memory studies emerged as an acceptable academic pursuit. The reasons for this explosion are at least partially connected to the recognition by social historians that certain human actions and collective aspects of events could not be completely explained by traditional historical sources alone. One turning point was the oral testimonies of Holocaust survivors at the 1961 trial of Adolf Eichmann which demonstrated in stark and tragic detail that evidence was much more than written documents. These testimonies made it increasingly clear that the Holocaust and other extreme human tragedies of the 20th century could not be understood solely through traditional documentation and archival evidence. The recognition that "testimonies, particularly when they are produced as part of larger cultural movements, express the discourse or discourses valued by society at the moment the witnesses tell their stories as much as they render an individual experience" (Wieviorka, 2006, p. xii) pushed academics and others to consider memory as a critical element for understanding both historical events and contemporary society and to acknowledge that collective memory adds unique and valuable perspectives in ways that would otherwise be missed.

Studying memory also offered the potential of understanding communities and cultures in more holistic ways that were not possible through traditional documentation. Less tangible "documents" such as oral testimonies, witnessing, trauma, personal and collective remembrances provided essential windows for more fully comprehending complex and often terrible events in human terms. Memory studies beginning in the late 20th century suddenly became paths to studying the undocumented and under-documented. As Jay Winter has pointed out,

> Whereas race, gender, and social class were foci of earlier waves of scholarship in cultural studies, now the emphasis is on a set of issues at the intersection of cultural history, literary studies, architecture, cognitive psychology, psychoanalysis, and many other disciplines besides. What they have in common is a focus on memory.
>
> (Winter, 2006, p. 54)

A critical aspect of memory is the way in which memory is communicated, both immediately and over time and generations. Connerton suggested that "to study the formation of memory is to study those acts of transfer that make remembering in common possible" (Connerton, 1989, p. 39). He proposed that this transfer happens in several ways – through commemoration and commemorative ceremonies, and through bodily practices which he described as being of two types, incorporated and inscribed. An incorporated practice is an action of transmission performed by the body. Transmission could be conscious, such as a handshake, or a culturally specific gesture generally understood by a particular community, such as a posture conveying dominance and power, which Connerton describes as "a mnemonic of the body" (p. 74). An inscribed practice refers to transmission through writing or other media forms. Connerton notes "The transition from an oral culture to a literate culture is a transition from incorporating practices to inscribing practices" (p. 75).

Cultural Memory

Connerton's memory duality between the inscribed (archival) and the incorporated (embodied) continues a binary thread running throughout the chapters of this book – a thread that continues to apply as both the incorporated and the inscribed function as components of cultural memory. Cultural memory has been defined as a constructed understanding of the past that is handed down through generations by text, oral traditions, monuments, commemorations and other modes of communication (National Geographic Society, 2022). It is the non-scribal tools of cultural memory, such as rituals, performative expressions, commemorations, traces and oral testimony, that give voice to communities that often stand apart from the documentary mainstream.

A related approach to cultural memory is suggested by Aleida Assmann, who argues that it is through culture that humans create a framework that transcends the life of the individual. She also frames cultural memory as a binary, making a distinction between two types of memory, active circulating memory (the canon) and passive historical memory (the archives). She describes both a tension and a continuing cyclical interchange between these two types of memory as society forgets, remembers and forgets again. Assmann considers the archives as the reference memory of society and a counterbalance to the necessarily lesser everyday working memory. She also regards the archives as a meta-memory, "a second order memory that preserves what has been forgotten" (Assmann, 2010, p. 106). As researchers find and interrogate forgotten memories, these memories move over into active collective memory. Seen from this perspective, the archives and the canon are continually dynamic and sensitive to social and historical shifts.

Together, Assmann asserts, the canon and the archives comprise cultural memory, that is, a memory that is dynamic and moving constantly between past and present.

Memory and Archives

While the memory theories articulated above make it clear that memory is closely connected to archives, archivists have tended to take a more cautious approach. On the one hand, they designate archives – as in national and other government repositories – as houses of memory; on the other, they contend that archives are the triggers and touchstones, or vehicles of memory but not memory itself (Millar, 2006, pp. 119, 121). And while the characterization of houses of memory as the treasures of our past to which archivists hold the keys is a persistent one, archivists have many other connections to memory that highlight it as one leg of the three-legged stool of archival values – evidence, memory and accountability.

While corporate memory and organizational memory are probably the memory tropes most familiar to archivists, memory and archives have been linked together and seen as sharing an implicit and significant relationship in many other aspects of archival processes. Not only do archivists collect, manage and preserve the "stuff" of memory, but, through the application of appraisal principles, they participate to a great extent in determining the continuity and perpetuation of memory.

The linking of memory and archives is a significant part of the archivist's responsibility. The records kept in houses of memory such as national archives are considered national memory, which shares an implicit relationship with cultural memory. Assmann referred to these national narratives as their "collective autobiography", pointing out that participating in national memory means understanding a nation's history and its symbols and celebrations. She concludes that cultural memory is based on two separate archival functions that support collective autobiography: "the presentation of a narrow selection of sacred texts, artistic masterpieces, or historic key events in a timeless framework; and the storing of documents and artifacts of the past" (Assmann, 2010, p. 101).

Nonetheless, despite its central function, memory occupies an uneasy space within the archives. On the one hand, memory has always been a basic tenet of archival value; on the other, while archival records can be characterized as triggers or touchstones for memory, memory itself remains fluid and intangible, presenting a condition that archivists have found difficult to reconcile with the fixity and tangible nature of traditional records.

The relationship between archives and memory strengthened significantly when Terry Cook identified memory as the second phase of a continuance of archival development. In a seminal essay outlining evolving paradigm shifts, he acknowledged that, "beyond evidence, archives also preserve memory. And they create memory" (Cook, 2013, p. 101). Paralleling Assmann's canon and archives, Cook positioned evidence and memory as interdependent even though they seem on the surface to be contradictory. He named evidence as the first archival paradigm shift and memory as the second. Identity and community were the third and fourth paradigms. These paradigms, united by evidence and memory, work together to support and encourage identity and community. Cook concluded that through "evidence-memory-identity practices, archival practice (and identity) can itself remain plural and diverse" (p. 102).

Memory and Community

As Cook implied, memory enters the cultural archives through multiple lenses, but, in more than any other way, it enters the archives through the lens of community. It is the community, whether local, national or international that determines what is to be remembered and what is to be forgotten. Each community constructs its own identity and claims its own cultural heritage. Both remembering and forgetting are ultimately dependent upon the people and communities who choose to remember or to forget. In the 21st century, as issues of cultural heritage are revisited and broadened in response to the demands of diverse constituencies, both memory and community have moved center stage with the increased recognition that "heritage turns out to be what people remember as significant" (Benton, 2010, p. 1).

Defining Communities

Pursuing the conjunction between communities and their records, several years ago I proposed the term "communities of records" to describe the interdependent and reciprocal relationship between communities and their records (Bastian, 2003). In a community of records, the community is both a record-creating entity and a memory frame that contextualizes the records it creates. At the time, I was thinking about a specific community, the United States Virgin Islands where the absence of the archival records of their colonial past mandated the forging of communal memory and identity through different kinds of (primarily intangible) records. But a community of records refers to any community at any level – national, local or institutional; and it refers to all of the records, archival and oral, tangible and intangible, scribal and embodied, generated by multiple layers of actions and interactions between and among the people and institutions within a community. The community and the records they create are one, mirroring each other as the community is both the creator and the provenance of its own records.

This initial construct of a community of records was enriched by Eric Ketelaar when he added memory to the equation, suggesting that "collective identity is based on the elective processes of memory, so that a given group recognises itself through its memory of a common past". He named community as a community of memory with a common embeddedness in the past: "The common past, sustained through time into the present, is what gives continuity, cohesion and coherence to a community" (Ketelaar, 2005, p. 54).

Memory, then, in equal measure with records, both defines a community and is defined by it. It is the collective memory of the past as well as the cultural memory of the present. As Assmann points out, the past and present inform and bind the community together, and, at the same time, this dynamic process creates memory for the future as well.

Communities as discrete entities exemplify the group lenses described by Halbwachs. These lenses are also components of the social provenance of a particular group or community. Understanding community as the context is, therefore, necessarily the first step in decoding a community's records and memories. But a critical corollary is that a community exists within multiple contexts. All communities live within a series of nested social provenances or contexts that might be both physical and intangible. A community may be contextualized within a particular place, but it may also be defined by a particular ethos, belief or characteristic.

The nature of a community is the key to understanding its memory and records; conversely, a community's memory and records can only be fully understood in relation to that community. "Community" may have multiple manifestations, but in both physical and virtual environments, we tend to understand communities as groups of individuals united around a set of commonalities. These commonalities may be varied and complex, but they generally coalesce around particular characteristics that include

- a common place or locality – shared physical geography or online spaces. A physical location could be a town, a village, or a nation;

online possibilities seem endless, but examples are Facebook pages and Twitter accounts.
- a common interest, belief or lifestyle – shared characteristics other than place that might fit into a variety of categories, such as religious beliefs, gender orientation, occupation, ethnicity, origins, activities such as sports, and civic organizations.
- a common purpose – shared events, missions, or attachment to a common idea or calling.

These commonalities inevitably overlap, so that each of us may belong to many different communities that fit into one or all of the categories above. Interacting with a community requires understanding its distinctive features, its reason for being, its identity and its place within wider society, which may be many and diverse. As Andrew Flinn notes, it is not a simple equation and involves both inclusion and exclusion:

> Definitions of what a 'community' might be are of course particularly complex and fluid and capable of multiple interpretations. Some definitions focus on locality, others on notions of shared beliefs or shared values producing a common purpose. Other discussions examine problems with who it is that seeks to define community and community membership, who determines who is included and who is excluded and whether it should be seen as an inclusive or as an exclusive and divisive concept.
>
> (Flinn, 2007, p. 153)

Community is often thought of as a local social system, but people living in the same location, joining the same organizations or enjoying the same activities do not necessarily interact or agree with one another. Even within organizations and activities, there may be many lenses. It is the relationships between people and their networks that are often considered the most significant aspect of community; in these relationships and networks, people share identity-forming narratives and stories that define an aspect of who they are, enabling them to make sense of the world through the lenses of those stories. Community is, therefore, all about people, their collective histories, memories and experiences. It is the place where they draw upon and reflect on cultural narratives and where they discover and reaffirm their collective memories.

The curative and corrective role of communities in adjusting and preserving memories, particularly those whose stories are untold in formal archives, has in recent decades been a driving force in the establishment of community archives. Both physical and online community archives are challenging formal archives as they pursue liberatory and social justice agendas dedicated to affirming and supporting the rights of all communities to their identities, narratives and cultural memories.

Community Archives

The Society of American Archivists defines Community Archives as, "documentation of a group of people that share common interests, and social, cultural and historical heritage, usually created by members of the group being documented and maintained outside of traditional archives" (Society of American Archivists, 2005-2022). They note that community archives are generally self-defined and often center around issues of social justice. They are created by the community itself, often by volunteers who may or may not be archivists, and may operate outside traditional archival institutions and often outside of traditional archival practices.

Community archives are significant signposts on the path toward cultural archives. They have been present in society in various forms for decades, although their origins are obscure. They have existed ever since groups of people have felt the need to affirm their identities, interests and commonalities within or apart from wider society. Historical societies, clubs, municipal organizations and independent collections are only a few of the many settings that have served to establish and express identity, whether of a group, a town, a region, an ethnicity, or of an affinity or a belief. All exist within multiple contexts that are key to understanding their memory lenses. For example, *Project Save* in Watertown, Massachusetts, is a photo-archives dedicated to documenting the Armenian heritage in the diaspora. As a community archives it functions locally for immigrant Armenian residents of Watertown and for the wider diaspora, but its provenance extends to the Armenian homeland and its genocidal history. It is dedicated to preserving the history and the culture of Armenians through photographs and the stories that those photographs tell (Project Save, n.d.). Similarly, the Herstory Archives in New York, founded as a community archives in 1972, sits within the ethos of New York and the feminist movement of the 1960s, as well as within the all-encompassing Gay Liberation Movement that triggered the need "to gather and preserve records of Lesbian lives and activities … [so that] future generations will have ready access to materials relevant to their lives" (Lesbian Herstory Archives, n.d.).

Over time, community archives have responded to and fulfilled a spectrum of community needs. From roles as chroniclers and documenters of community engagement in war, as counter-narratives to official history books and public culture institutions, to social justice advocacy, community archives have reacted to the imperatives of their time. Flinn and his colleagues note that "[t]he defining characteristic of a community archives is the active participation of the community in documenting and making accessible the history of their particular group and/or locality on their own terms" (Flinn et al., 2009, p. 73). This central quality of ownership has meant that, to a great extent, it is the group that defines the contents of its archives, and the forms of documentation are specific to the group's needs and wishes.

Technology has been a significant driver of community archives. Ever since Howard Rheingold introduced the term "virtual community" in 1993, having established a pioneering online community in 1985, The WELL (Rheingold, 1993), digital technologies have significantly expanded the boundaries of "community" and the ability of people to interact within online networks. No longer location-dependent, online communities function in virtual environments every day, through both constructed websites and social media, using networks designed specifically to foster community. Connerton's suggestion that memory and collective memory are about communication and the acts of transfer that make that possible was noted earlier in this chapter. Whether physical or virtual, community archives are significant vehicles for both collective and cultural memory.

The Web has not so much redefined the concept of community as created the possibility of extending it. No longer location-dependent, digital community archives can reach out to wide diasporas. Some community archives have both a physical and online presence; others are completely online. The Black Cultural Archives in the United Kingdom, founded in 1981, for example, is physically located in London but, through its online presence is also a national heritage center dedicated to collecting, preserving and celebrating the histories of African and Caribbean people in Britain (Black Cultural Archives, 2022). The History Project, an LGBTQ+ archive located in Boston, reaches out to the whole of New England through its extensive website (The History Project, 2019). Other community archives, such as the South Asian American Digital Archive (SAADA), are fully online and reach out to a widespread community. SAADA's mission is to create "a more inclusive society by giving voice to South Asian Americans through documenting, preserving, and sharing stories that represent their unique and diverse experiences" (South Asian American Digital Archives, 2008–2022).

Significantly, these and other community archives, which are often set up and run primarily by volunteers, tend to work outside of the archival box and do not follow traditional archival practices. While their collections may include traditional archival materials, they also include a range of other types of materials and may be arranged and organized in ways that facilitate use by their community, rather than in record groups and series. The Black Cultural Archives includes not only manuscript material but also ephemera, artifacts, books, newspapers, music and art work. The Lesbian Herstory Archives has a vast array of information in many forms, including T-shirts, banners, oral history and zines, all of which are organized for easy access.

Community and Memory in the Cultural Archives

Cultural memory is at the heart of community archives. Through a variety of tangible and intangible materials and expressions, community archives not only confirm but also restore memory; they not only present identity but also invite communities to affirm identity. Although community archives are not the only vehicle for cultural memory, they offer a model for repositories to include a wide variety of cultural expressions within an archival matrix and offer clues about how cultural archives can fuse traditional documentation and cultural expressions.

The Juluwarlu Group of Western Australia established an online community in 2000, bringing the dispersed communities of the Yindjibarndi people together. In addition to a wide range of cultural memory and cultural identity activities, the online community's website offers a large searchable archives of recordings, videos, film and photographs. By focusing on heritage, history and language, it engages in "effectively empowering Aboriginal people in our cultural, artistic, social, economic, political and environmental pursuits" (Juluwarlu Group Aboriginal Corporation, 2015–2022, Our story).

Significantly, the website focuses on intangible heritage in an extensive section on beliefs that includes Creation stories, law, a calendar of the seasons, plants and animals, illustrated by sound recordings, photographs and narratives. The importance of cultural sensitivity is evident in the request that users of the website respect the memories and voices of Yindjibarndi Elders captured in the photographs, words, films and recordings accessible through the site, with a note to visitors on the opening webpage, " our website contains photographs, words, documentary films and recordings of the voices of the Old People who have gone before us. Please be respectful of their memory" (Juluwarlu Group Aboriginal Corporation, 2015–2022).

Intangible heritage is also a central feature of small community archives in Thailand. The maintenance of spiritual and traditional practices alongside artifacts such as textiles, palm-leaf manuscripts and photographs was a focus in a study in four Thai communities. The report on the study suggests that "intangible heritage is more likely to be sustained than tangible heritage", because the community can sustain, recreate or even re-invent traditional practices, whereas material objects may deteriorate over time if the community doesn't have the resources to maintain them (Simionica, 2020, p. 86). Reflecting on Thai practices, the author encourages Western community archives to "recognise both the tangible and intangible heritage of local communities to include folksong, crafting, dance and performance, and the centrality of memory (especially orality) to most community archive endeavours" (p. 92).

Memory/Archives – Together At Last

Acknowledging cultural memory and the expressions of memory as powerful records of a community is the first step towards archiving the memory of a community. As the examples above have shown, communities find ways to make the intangible knowable and to blend the scribal and the oral. Affirming the diversity of memory formats, the UNESCO Memory of the World program suggests that cultural memory is embodied within objects, documents and artifacts and that the memory is not separate from the archives (UNESCO Memory of the World, n.d.). From this standpoint, a wide array of physical artifacts – monuments and memorials, as well as texts – are the embodiment of memory. While memory itself may be an abstract, people and communities make those abstracts tangible. Recent innovations in digital technologies are bringing memory and the archives even closer together and changing the ways that memory is archived. Increasingly technical advances, smartphones, social media and crowd-sourcing are enabling instant documentation and the creation of instant archives of memory.

I offer two examples:

- The Syrian Archive collects, verifies and preserves visual documentation of human rights violations in Syria. Using open-source software, the Archive posts a wide variety of materials from over 35,000 reliable sources, including journalists, field reporters and human rights organizations. Much of the documentation is from

civilians and collected from YouTube videos and other social media and news outlets. Their ongoing project, *(Re-)Humanization of the Syrian Digital Memory,* explores how "civilians' documentary practices and experiences have significantly contributed to the production of multi-source digital testimonies within diverse and constantly transforming local, social, political and organisational contexts" (Syrian Archive, n.d.). The archives, accessible through the Syrian Archive's website, include testimonies, videos and photographs that provide evidence of atrocities.
- During the 2011 uprising in Egypt, the Mosireen Collective, which was part of the protest movement, set up a media tent in Cairo's Tahrir Square to collect videos and films that civilians were taking on their cameras and smartphones. The intent was to collect evidence of the events and to counter the images of empty streets broadcast on state media. Eventually, images and footage were collected from all over Egypt. Although this material was never used, as the uprising was violently quelled, the Mosireen Collective created the 858 Archive, which presents raw footage showing the history of the uprising from thousands of perspectives. It consists of 1,662 video images, each randomly capturing and witnessing a particular moment of the eighteen days of the Tahrir Square revolution. The images are searchable by keywords; together they form a powerful visual testimony of the uprising's events (858 An Archive of Resistance, n.d.).

With the immediacy of a smartphone, an image captured in real-time becomes an instant memory and an instant record. A moment is documented almost simultaneously with its memory creation. Through this instant creation, memory suddenly has a new agenda and a new presence in the archives because, while technology might memorialize and document an action, the visual memory also becomes a witness, memorializing and sustaining a concern for social justice.

Digital technologies offer possibilities that have helped move memory closer to events. This compression of time enables the creation of dynamic archives in which memory and records seem to occur almost simultaneously – an affordance utilized by both archivists and digital humanists. No longer solely the province of academics, memory is now a societal activity. Crowd-sourced, citizen-inspired, technology-driven memorializing has become a critical activity both for the collective and the individual; it has become an aspect of identity and community as well as of justice.

Conclusion: Collective Memory Redux

In November 2020, the bronze bust of Danish King Christian IX, erected with much fanfare in 1909, was removed from Emancipation Park, the public gardens at the center of Charlotte Amalie on St. Thomas. It was replaced with The Conch Shell Blower, a statue of a Black man blowing a conch shell, a call to freedom and a clear reference to the collective memory of the 1848 Emancipation rebellion on St. Croix that led to the abolition of slavery in the Danish colony. Initially, the Conch Shell Blower was placed at the Park's periphery, but on July 4, 2022, the statue was moved to the center, rededicated and renamed the Freedom Statue. Speakers at the ceremony noted that it signaled an official change in the historical narrative of the park and in the community's desire to take control of its own destiny (Pancham, 2022, Statue rededication).

Similar emancipation monuments are prominently placed in many Caribbean nations and territories, often replacing monuments to the colonizer. Exploring these emancipation monuments, Lawrence Brown notes that "in each society it [emancipation] has been remembered as the founding moment of national identity and citizenship". But this memory is mutable, whereas monuments in stone or metal were intended to have a fixed meaning. Shifting reactions to them over time "reveal that perceptions of the Caribbean past have always been fluid, divisive and contested … [and] have remained focal points for present debates on the meaning of that freedom" (Brown, 2002, p. 93).

Part of the collective memory, monuments and memorials are meant to be read as visual texts. In their mutability, they support both the canon and the archives, as well as the historical event and its current meaning. "Memorials, like statues, are susceptible to changes taking place in society" (Aarons, 2022, p. 62); the fate of King Christian, now relocated to the St. Thomas Historical Trust Museum, and the progressive elevation of the Conch Shell Blower to Freedom Statue speak to this fluidity.

The relocation of the Conch Shell Blower to the center of Emancipation Park was meant to reaffirm the critical fact that in 1848 the enslaved of St. Croix took their destiny into their own hands and, after an organized march across the island to the Danish Fort Frederik, demanded their freedom from Governor General von Scholten. The emancipation story and the legends surrounding its organizer and leader, "General" Buddhoe, are enshrined in the collective memories of Virgin Islanders and reinforced by statues of Buddhoe on all three of the US Virgin Islands. Significantly, when the role of Buddhoe was brought into question in the late 1990s by a Danish/American researcher who suggested that this hero might have been complicit with the Danish military, Virgin Islanders deliberately chose to discount this possibility, not only because they could not verify it in records they had no access to, but also because they recognized Buddhoe's significance as a folk hero, a symbol of emancipation and a central part of the Virgin Islands collective memory.[1]

Collective memory is a powerful cultural expression that functions as a record over time. Like the sand in the Synagogue that may speak slightly differently to each generation of congregants as they move from Sephardic to Ashkenazi and from European to American, and the emancipation memorials that shift from Danish colonialism to the agency of the descendants of the former enslaved, the narrative of collective memory may adjust and modify but still retain its essential and persistent core meaning. Seen as records in the cultural archives, both the sand and the statue fulfill the requirement of persistence that defines a record. Both also exist within well-defined contexts or provenances that include not only the lenses of their particular communities but also the contexts of the wider community of St. Thomas and its complex history.

The longitudinal quality of collective memory, its evolution over time, the constancy of its core and the contextual framework through which it is viewed give it integrity and reliability as cultural evidence. Memory, an intangible quality that manifests through tangible objects, adds depth and authenticity to the cultural archives. Cultural memory is a significant component of a cultural archive. Community archives are demonstrating its centrality and increasingly digital technologies offer strategies for implementation. The final chapter continues to explore the potential of technology to unify the tangible and the intangible and considers the role of the archivist in creating archival equity.

Note

1 For an in-depth analysis of this situation and the sources, see J. A. Bastian. "Taking custody, giving access: A postcustodial role for a new century," *Archivaria*, 53 (2002): 76–93.

References

Aarons, E. (2022). Archives 'cast in stone': Memorials as memory. In J. Aarons, J.A. Bastian & S.H. Griffin (Eds.) *Archiving Caribbean identity: Records, community and memory* (pp. 49–63). Routledge.

Assmann, A. (2010). Canon and archive. In A. Erll & A. Nünning (Eds.) *A companion to cultural memory studies* (pp. 97–108). De Gruyter.

Bastian, J.A. (2003). *Owning memory, how a Caribbean community lost its archives and found its history*. Libraries Unlimited.

Benton, B. (2010). Introduction. In T. Benton (Ed.) *Understanding heritage and memory* (pp. 1–5). Manchester University Press.

Black Cultural Archives (2022). *The home of Black British history*. https://blackculturalarchives.org/

Brown, L. (2002). Monuments to freedom, monuments to nation: The politics of emancipation and remembrance in the Eastern Caribbean. *Slavery and Abolition*, 23(3), pp. 93–116.

Connerton, P. (1989). *How societies remember*. Cambridge University Press.

Cook, T. (2013). Evidence, memory, identity, and community: Four shifting archival paradigms. *Archival Science,* 13, pp. 95–120.

858, an Archive of Resistance (n.d.). https://858.ma/

Flinn, A. (2007). Community histories, community archives: Some opportunities and challenges. *Journal of the Society of Archivists,* 28(2), pp. 151–176.

Flinn, A., Stevens, M. & Shepherd, E. (2009). Whose memories, whose archives?: Independent community archives, autonomy and the mainstream. *Archival Science,* 9, pp. 71–86.

Halbwachs, M. (1992). *On collective memory* (L. Coser, Ed. & Trans.). University of Chicago Press (Original work published 1925).

Hebrew Congregation of St. Thomas (n.d.). Our historic synagogue. https://synagogue.vi/our-historic-synagogue/

Juluwarlu Group Aboriginal Corporation (2015–2022). Our story. https://juluwarlu.com.au/our-story/

Ketelaar, E. (2005). Sharing: Collected memories in communities of records. *Archives and Manuscripts,* 33(1), pp. 44–61.

Levesque-Schaefer, E. (n.d.). *Lesbian herstory archives*. https://lesbianherstoryarchives.org/

Millar, L. (2006). Touchstones: Considering the relationship between memory and archives. *Archivaria,* 61, pp. 105–126.

National Archives Catalog. Virgin Islands SP St. Thomas Synagogue – Beracha Veshalom Vegemiluth Hasadim (1997). *National Register Nomination*. https://catalog.archives.gov/id/131518967

National Geographic Society (2022). *Cultural memory*. https://www.nationalgeographic.org/encyclopedia/cultural-memory/

Pancham, A. (2022, July 4). Statue rededication helps change narrative of Emancipation Day. *The St. Thomas Source*. https://stthomassource.com/content/2022/07/04/statue-rededication-helps-change-narrative-of-emancipation-day/

Project Save Photograph Archive (n.d.). Who we are. https://projectsave.org/who-we-are/

Rheingold, H. (1993). *The virtual community: Homesteading on the electronic frontier*. Basic Books.

Russell, N. (2006). Collective memory before and after Halbwachs. *French Review,* 79(4), pp. 792–804.

Simionica, K.N. (2020). Self-documentation of Thai communities: Reflective thoughts on the Western concept of community archives. In J.A. Bastian & A. Flinn (Eds.) *Community archives, community spaces; Heritage, memory and identity* (pp. 79–95). Facet.

Society of American Archivists (2005–2022). *Dictionary of archives terminology*, https://dictionary.archivists.org/

South Asian American Digital Archives (2008–2022). *SAADA, mission.* https://www.saada.org/mission

Syrian Archive (n.d.). *Syrian digital memory.* https://syrianarchive.org/en/memory

The History Project (2019). *Documenting, preserving, and sharing New England's LGBTQ history.* https://historyproject.org/index.php/about

UNESCO Memory of the World (n.d.). Records to remember. https://artsandculture.google.com/story/ugXBF8rpN5R8_Q

Wieviorka, A. (2006). *The era of the witness* (J. Stark, Trans.). Cornell University Press (Originally published, 1999).

Winter, J. (2006). Notes on the memory boom: War, remembrance and the uses of the past. In D. Bell (Ed.). *Memory, trauma and world politics* (pp. 54–73). Palgrave Macmillan.

6 In the Cultural Archives

Introduction

Thinking about culture means thinking about binaries. The cultural binaries throughout these chapters are striking – intangible and tangible, fluid and static, oral and scribal, performative and textual. Often presented as stark opposites, they channel human expressions into dichotomies. While these opposites recognize many and varied modes of communication, they are ultimately only a hindrance to cultural sensitivities. They offer convenient and easy ways to categorize, to reject and to other, but in doing so dismiss opportunities for acknowledging the many ways in which people and communities express and record their histories and their identities. As F. Gerald Ham exhorted archivists in the 1970s,

> [T]he archivist must realize that he can no longer abdicate his role in this demanding intellectual process of documenting culture. … [I]f he is passive, uninformed, with a limited view of what constitutes the archival record, the collections that he acquires will never hold up a mirror for mankind. And if we are not holding up that mirror, if we are not helping people understand the world they live in, and if this is not what archives is all about, then I do not know what it is we are doing that is all that important.
>
> (Ham, 1975, p. 13)

The challenge of the cultural archives is, to a great extent, the challenge of bridging the binaries: how to describe, access and preserve the intangible; how to capture the repertoire; how to anchor the fluid. But bridging the binaries is not the only challenge. The more critical challenge lies in adjusting the archival mindset and ensuring that archivists are willing and able to reach beyond the silos of the

DOI: 10.4324/9781003091813-7

dichotomies and tear them down in order to create an archival equity that accepts all records. In that equity, the textual and the performative, the oral and the scribal exist side by side within one expansive archival framework. Australian archivist Sue McKemmish has noted that records may take many forms: "Thus society's Archive in the very broadest sense includes 'oral and written records, literature, landscape, dance, art, the built environment and artefacts' insofar as they provide traces of social, cultural and organizational activity, that evidence and memorialize individual and collective lives" (McKemmish et al., 2019, p. 284).

Previous chapters have suggested that the binaries can work together in tandem; for example, written choreographic details of a dance performance can be stored together with visual representations and musical recordings of that performance, and a nation's textual records can be linked with oral recordings of its folk heritage. The incorporation of two components of a binary within an archive is also eased and encouraged by digital technologies.

This chapter explores these two challenges: the uniting of the binaries by using digital technologies to bring together seemingly irreconcilable opposites, and adjusting archival thinking to accommodate this unification. The marrying of opposites also suggests that digital technologies are transforming archives from formidable bureaucratic spaces into global gathering spaces that include the re-visioning of archival practice and expansion of principles to create archival equity. Re-visioning the archival mindset as well may be a natural outcome of these digital re-visionings, which are driven by both public and institutional demand.

Digital Archives

Media scholar Niels Brügger argues that "all digital media come with their own digitality – that is, a specific way of being digital". He uses the term "digitality" for the different ways in which a digital medium creates a media artifact. He divides digital media into three groups; digitized media, born-digital media, and reborn digital media (media "that have been collected and preserved, and that have been changed during this process" (Brugger, 2018, p. 5).

Archivists have been working with these three groups of digital media since the early production of electronic records in the mid-20th century, work which inspired Gerald Ham's presidential address to the Society of American Archivists quoted above. Today archivists continue to contend with records in all of the formats that Brügger identifies. The challenges of these digital formats give rise to new and creative archival configurations which simultaneously change and enhance the ways in which archives are collected, organized, preserved and accessed.

Digital archives initially referred to born-digital records preserved by institutions and organizations but evolved to include collections of both born-digital and digitized materials (Theimer, 2015, pp. 157–159). Digital archives is also an umbrella term for a website that serves as a portal for accessing the digitized collections of one or more institutions. Many archives consider their digital archives to be the website through which they provide access to their digitized and born-digital collections as well as to materials from other sources, and "it is this usage, rather than an archives or collection of born-digital materials, that currently appears to be the most prevalent" (Theimer, p. 157). This book uses the term in this sense.

From the late 20th century, several innovative archival projects demonstrated the access and research potential of digitizing records. Utilizing the newly developed World Wide Web, the award-winning *The Valley of the Shadow* was launched in the 1990s by the University of Virginia which used its collections of diaries, letters and other records to create digital archives of the lives of two communities before, during and after the American Civil War (University of Virginia Libraries, 1993–2007). In 2002, the Center for New Media at George Mason University launched *The September 11 Digital Archive* (Roy Rosenzweig Center for History and New Media, 2002–2022). In addition to documenting and preserving all aspects of the tragedy that unfolded in New York on September 11, 2001, the primary goal was to create "a free public space for people to contribute their stories and to allow them to deposit the rich array of digital evidence that they had created personally or received electronically" (Brier & Brown, 2011, p. 101). Demonstrating the capacity for user participation and interactivity, this site became one of individual and national mourning, hosting over 72,000 personal stories and over 6,000 images (Roy Rosenzweig Center for History and New Media, 2021).

Living Archives

Digital archives that can be navigated with flexibility and are interactive and participatory are rapidly evolving, engaging with and interpreting archival collections through a variety of media and in different formats as well as encouraging the creation of new material. With their focus on wide public access and on visual and often aural representation, many of these archives describe themselves as living archives. Primarily with a solid base in an archival collection, living archives, as demonstrated in the examples below, offer insights into the potential of digital archives to bridge the boundaries

One definition of living archives is a collection "of materials presented in a way that allows for the expression, exhibition, documentation and preservation of a sentiment or movement in a particular community" (UC San Diego Library, 2017). Other definitions vary, depending upon the institution proposing the definition, but most agree on components that emphasize the archives as dynamic and fluid presentations and that unite the memory of the institution with contemporary practices and with environments "that connect the organisation, curation and transmission of memory with present-bound creative, performative, and participatory processes" (Sabiescu, 2020, p. 497).

A living archive primarily matches Brügger's third group of digital media – reborn digital media that have been collected and preserved and have been changed in the process – but it could also include material specifically digitized and born-digital material that has been incorporated. Not all digital archives are called living archives, but, increasingly, they demonstrate levels of interactivity, user participation and multi-media approaches that put them into the category of living archives.

Tell Us How UC It; A Living Archive for Student Activism at UC San Diego, an online space created by four women in the UC San Diego Library to document student activism, proposes three parts for living archives:

- **Historical Narrative:** a timeline of historical artifacts and accounts documenting the progression of a movement
- **Current Reflections:** creative works by current members of a community that offer an expression of community sentiments and experiences at that time
- **Real-time Feedback**: feedback about the exhibit or movement as a whole, whereby preserving in-the-moment responses allows reflections of the past to converge with vital expressions of current sentiment (UC San Diego Library, 2017)

These guidelines on documenting social justice issues advocate components of living archives that focus on the community as well as on creating an archive. They include documenting events "in-the-moment", creating context for that moment through historical archival documentation and including public responses and reflections as part of the documentation. The archives are living because they are continuously formed – they are in motion. There is a sense that a historical record is being created.

This in-the-moment urgency to document and preserve history as it is happening has become a powerful tool in the service of social justice, assisted and encouraged by grassroots websites such as *Documenting the Now*, which not only develop open-source tools but also advise and educate on the sensitive issues involved in the ethical management of content, collecting, use and privacy (Documenting the Now, n.d.). *A People's Archive of Police Violence in Cleveland*, for example, encourages users to contribute their own stories but also features posters, photographs and oral testimonies. The creators of the website write, "May this online space for healing, accountability, and justice continue to exist so long as the national crisis of police violence persists" (A Peoples Archive of Police Violence in Cleveland, 2022, Purpose).

In addition to documenting social justice issues, living archives are leveraging technology to explore cultural heritage as a social resource, to document and facilitate social change and to create cultural awareness and collective collaboration. Interpretations of exactly what a living archive is differs, but all demonstrate the potential for technology to bring tangible and intangible records together. The following examples illustrate some of the many different versions of living archives.

- *Circus Oz Living Archive* (Circus Oz Living Archive, 2014), a project that investigated the deployment and formation of digital images and networked technologies in the performing arts, first made its website accessible to the public in 2014. This experiment in bringing complex and dynamic performance archives to life in a digital space utilized the physical records of a renowned Australian animal-free circus, Circus Oz, as its case study.

Circus Oz began in 1978 as a contemporary animal-free circus which blended traditional circus skills with other performance arts. The developers of the *Circus Oz Living Archive* gathered the archives of Circus Oz – the videos, letters, posters, photographs and all the records of the life of the circus and its performances. The website they developed not only brings the circus and the archives to life in a digital environment, but recasts the archive itself. As one of the project partners suggests, "the digital archive in the performing arts context should best be seen not as a fixed and static record, in opposition to the original live performance event, but as 'an enduring, evolving digital event' in its own right"(Carlin & Vaughan, 2015, p.4).[1]

What makes these archives living archives is not just the repurposing of videos of old performances and the digitizing of images and records, but the digital fitting together and positioning of all the pieces of a circus in such a way that makes it seem like the user is witnessing a performance in real time. The archives come alive, not only as a dynamic simulation of a circus, but as a performance of its textual artifacts. As one of the contributors to the book about the archive notes, the flatness of the actual archives where items and collections are described uniformly is made three dimensional by the networking capability of technology: "When digitised, a *properly networked* archive can be conceptualised as a system to enable a multiplicity of virtual relations, that is, a meta-system" (Miles, 2015, p. 47). Creating a network of relationships within a circumscribed context retains the internal provenance of the records and their archival integrity, key aspects of archival practice and thinking

The website launched in 2014 included documentation of performances, interviews, rehearsals, documentaries and promotional footage from the 1970s to 2012. In 2020 *Circus Oz Living Archive* was revived and is now available for public access, with the promise of new material being added.

- The *Kaldor Public Art Projects* first brought innovative contemporary arts projects to the Australian public in the 1960s, fulfilling the vision of philanthropist, John Kaldor. The first project, in 1969, was Christo and Jeanne-Claude's iconic Wrapped Coast at Sydney's Little Bay. In the 2000s the Projects developed the *Living Archives* to recall its many presentations through photographs and personal recollections. The *Living Archives* "animates the Kaldor Public Art Projects archives with the memories of those who experienced our projects firsthand" (Kaldor Arts Project, 2022, *Living Archives*). The living archives re-uses and re-animates previous exhibits by assembling personal memories, digitized artworks and documents describing the installations.
- In 2012, to celebrate the 100th anniversary of composer John Cage's birth, the New York Public Library initiated *John Cage Unbound, A Living Archive.* This online multi-media website made use of the Library's collections of Cage's music, manuscripts, films of performances, program notes and other material. Musicians were invited to upload videos of their own interpretations of Cage's work. The project's vision was to make Cage's music relevant to a new generation of students, performers and teachers by inviting re-interpretations of his music. The objective, according to the

curator of the living archives, was to present "an online record of John Cage's work and its evolving impact on music and performance" (Statham, 2015, p. 159).[2] The archive's accumulation of videos of musical performances by many different ensembles and individuals fulfilled that objective and extended the Library's archival collections. This living archive is primarily a sound archive that brings the archived printed music to life and is a place that encourages the continued performance and understanding of Cage's music by new generations of musicians.

- In Stanford University's *Living Archive of William McDonough*, a collaborative project between the architect and the university, "living" is interpreted as working and communicating with an individual who is alive. The website gives access to his papers, photographs chronicling McDonough's life, work spaces and buildings. It links to videos of McDonough's speeches and lectures. The *Living Archive of William McDonough* claims that it "is a whole new approach to archiving. By archiving in real-time we are able to create a complete picture of McDonough's work, connections and global impact" (Stanford University Libraries, 2022). It is envisaged that the website's content will change as the archives grows and as the public engages with McDonough through Twitter and LinkedIn. This living archives involves the fluidity of engaging with the life of a living person
- *The Living Archive: Extinction Stories from Oceania* encourages visitors to contribute their stories about what extinction means and how it matters in their lives and locations. In this multimedia space are posted photographs, video and sound recordings that document a wide variety of animals, plants and landscapes in danger of extinction and exploitation. An interactive map of Oceania contextualizes and locates the islands in the Pacific Ocean and highlights "the varied, and often unequal, ways in which the decline and disappearance of irreplaceable aspects of our living world is shaping the contours of local lives and places, impacting on cultural practices, livelihoods, and connections to land and sea" (The Living Archive, n.d., About).
- *Living Archive: An AI Performance Experiment* uses artificial intelligence to mine the extensive video archives of choreographer Wayne McGregor and generates animated archives of dance movements. In this experiment with his video archives by McGregor and the Google Arts and Culture Lab, an AI tool creates a live dialogue between dancers and McGregor's work. McGregor found that "one of the most fascinating aspects of the

> technology is that it can learn and recreate the particular style of a dancer … [I]t can go some way toward capturing their [dancers] creative identity" (Leprince-Ringuet, 2018).

Living archives, underpinned by archival collections, add real-time elements to historical records and, through various ongoing participatory activities, enable new archival material to be created. They exemplify the interplay of past and present in Aleida Assmann's theoretical framework of the cultural archives. The canon (working memory) and the archives (reference memory) create a continuing interchange between current and historical memory, which support and enhance one another in an endless cycle. In this cycle "both the active and the passive realms of cultural memory are anchored in institutions that are not closed against each other but allow for mutual influx and reshuffling" (Assmann, 2010, p. 106). Although each site introduced in the examples above differs slightly in its interpretation of living archives, fluidity, public participation, change and presentness are constant components.

In addition to the digital projects whose websites officially announce them to be living archives, many other digital projects engage with archival records in ways that distinguish them as such. Among these are government archival sites which give new life to historical documents on the dynamic web. As the web has provided archives with digital possibilities, archivists are bringing fresh interpretations to documents as they and their users engage in new ways with materials that previously resided only in record boxes. One example is *Discovering Anzacs,* a website created by the National Archives of Australia and Archives New Zealand to commemorate 100 years since the beginning of World War I. Users are invited to "explore a diverse selection of government records about Australians and New Zealanders in World War I and the Boer War" (National Archives of Australia, n.d.) and to contribute stories to the site and to listen to them. Videos, timelines, photographs and maps enhance personal records. This website is continually being augmented as its users add new records, which in turn constitute an expansion of the underpinning archives.

Digital Gatherings

The flexible environment and possibilities of the web that accommodate both the tangible and the intangible are particularly hospitable to gatherings of people concerned with creating, establishing, preserving and perpetuating their own cultural heritage and traditions. Indigenous communities have been at the forefront of developing digital sites that enable access to the oral traditions, world views, and landscapes that are both central to their heritage and also protect that heritage. The website of Juluwarlu Group of Western Australia discussed in Chapter 5 is only one example of a website that brings dispersed communities together; there are many others.

Mukurtu, an access platform managed by the University of Washington Center for Digital Scholarship and Curation and designed in collaboration with an Indigenous community, was developed in 2007 specifically for the records requirements of Indigenous communities, including protected access and curatorial care. One of the platform's co-founders, Kimberly Christen, explains: "The salient point is that the communities themselves decide together how best to share and circulate their cultural materials. Mukurtu allows local communities (however defined) to use their own protocols for the viewing, circulation, use, and access to cultural materials to be embedded into their community archive" (Christen, 2015, p. 5). Ownership and control of the narrative is a critical feature, as it is in all community archives.

Digital Interventions

Video essays that engage archival records with multimedia offer another approach to actualizing the intangible. Often presented as part of art installations, these videos can also be considered as inserts into archival collections. Two examples of recent experiments focus on specific documents but both suggest larger archival contexts, the history of Hawaii as well as Polish occupation and emigration in World War II.

Liliuokalani, Archival Experimentations, described as "an experiment in interactive biography and participatory transmedia", tells the haunting story of the last queen of Hawaii, who was exiled within her own country, imprisoned in her own palace, yet devoted her life to the translation of the Hawaiian chants that tell the story of these islands. This video essay uses archival photographs and words from the Queen's memoir. In the background is the song "Aloha Oe" ("Farewell to Thee"), written by Liliuokalani while she was detained as a political prisoner. The author notes that the essay "involved video-remixing the original, open-source images of the Queen from the Hawaiian Governments online archives. As such, this conceptual piece represents an experiment in the surface wanderings over art, history, anthropology, interactivity and digitalia" (Ward, July 25, 2020).

Exile to Leeds 6 – The Palka Diaries is a short video essay based on a diary that tells the story of the director's Polish father exiled to Siberia in 1940. As the son retraces his father's journey, he reads appropriate excerpts as his train moves through Russia. Maps tracing the route and scenes of Russia are superimposed on the diary pages and aspects of the father's experiences are intermingled with stories told to his son. The background noise of the train brings the diary to life, and video and images convey a sense of the journey, as does the landscape, present and past (Palka, 2020).

It's All in the Mind

Although digital technologies have opened the door to methods and techniques for bringing the binaries together, can archivists reconcile oral traditions, embodied performances, and the artifacts of memory with their mental model of an archival record? Over the past two decades, there have been calls within the archival community to abandon traditional archival frameworks that privilege the textual, the tangible and the master narratives of the powerful in favor of more inclusive models.

This book proposes a different approach to archival equity. It suggests that considering the cultural expressions of communities as their archival records requires expanding the archival mindset beyond the textual and the static to encompass the oral, the fluid, and the dynamic. It proposes that an archive that recognizes many formats and modes of expression as records of heritage, history and identity and does so within traditional archival principles would truly hold up a mirror for mankind. This is not to suggest that Western archival frameworks could or should be applied to the cultural expressions of non-Western communities, or that one size fits all in the cultural universe. Rather, this book suggests that archival principles such as provenance, order and internal relationships, custody/ownership, and archival values such as evidence, memory and identity are broadly applicable if imagined expansively and globally. Archival thinking goes beyond traditional archives alone.

Archival thinking involves thinking about many areas of knowledge in an archival way. Joanna Sassoon conflates archeology and geology with landscape and memory as she demonstrates how these disciplines can be thought of archivally. She asks "What if we recognised the common archival thinking which underpins studies of landscapes, archaeological materials, the built environment and geological evidence and see our natural partners as the heritage sector." She suggests that this is a natural progression, because "archives are part of a broader cultural system in which heritage is seen as the umbrella" (Sassoon, 2007, p. 45).

Mike Jones continues this meditation on archival thinking by identifying the ways of thinking. about what is central to archival practice. These include the following:

- the belief that the **order** in which material is kept and used contributes to its meaning;
- an interest in determining and capturing information about **provenance**;
- a recognition that the **context** in which records are created and managed (including people, organisational structures, concepts, places and other entities) is essential to understanding their content;
- an understanding that these are all part of a **system of relationships and connections** which helps provide **meaning** to each individual component, and;
- a focus on **sustainable practice** to help ensure these systems are documented and managed effectively so as to remain accessible and understandable over long periods of time (emphasis mine) (Jones, 2016, p. 213).

Order, provenance, context, relationships, meaning, sustainability – these principles and values are all critical to archival practice. Throughout this book, they have also been applied to the cultural expressions that have been analyzed in each chapter. Oral traditions, landscapes, performances, monuments, and memories also involve these principles and values, and all might be considered as the records of their particular communities. Thinking archivally should include the modes, the styles, and the formats by which all societies express their history, their identity, and their sense of themselves.

Whether digital or analog, bridging the binaries and changing the archival mindset are part of the same ongoing endeavor, the one leading to the other. Dismissing the dichotomies and flattening the cultural playing field to include a wide variety of global cultural expressions and cultural knowlege requires a change in perspective as well as the courage to do so. Digitization is a major enabler of this change. As the examples above illustrate, there are many ways to think about what an archive could be, many ways to reconfigure archival materials, and many ways to describe, present and create access to knowledge. The digital environment suddenly makes it possible to bring the oral and the scribal, the performative and the static, the intangible and the tangible together in harmony and in unity.

Conclusion: Holding up a Mirror

In the 1970s, Ham, calling upon archivists to embrace electronic recordkeeping, identified the archival mission as holding up a "mirror for mankind". His words have resonated across the decades. Although electronic recordkeeping has been largely embraced in the 21st century, the archival mission that Ham espoused remains unfulfilled. Until all peoples and cultures are represented in the archives, archives only hold up a mirror to a select segment of mankind. How the mirror can reflect all of mankind and why it should do so has been the primary focus of this book.

In the Introduction, I note that, in order to be relevant, meaningful and enduring in a global society, archives must represent everyone and have the mechanisms and the strategies to do that. I ask how archives that consider intangible cultural expressions and tangible documentation equally as records can be legitimately and seamlessly accommodated and subsumed within archival practice. The examples from folklore, landscape, performance, community and memory throughout these chapters suggest why cultural expressions are also archival records and how the tangible and the intangible can be united.

Digital technologies offer methods and techniques, but it is in archival thinking that emphasizes internal values rather than external formats that solutions may be found. Uniting the performative and the scribal, and the tangible and the intangible in broad categories of cultural and archival heritage with no dichotomies, no silos and no qualifying reservations is a goal that may be difficult to achieve, but is well worth the journey. Many archivists are already taking that journey.

As a final example of the possibilities in archival unity, I offer this vignette from the Caribbean island of Montserrat in which the repertoire and the archives, and the oral and the scribal, combine to tell a complete narrative.

A micro-history combines oral and archival records as part of an effort to document Montserrat society. Archivist Gracelyn Cassell tells the story of an ordinary laborer, Thomas 'Sugar' Riley. Born in 1907, Thomas 'Sugar' grew up in colonial (British) Montserrat. His life story and memory of endurance and survival in the canefields of Santo Domingo and the cotton fields of Montserrat also tells the story of the struggle and poverty in the island in the mid-20th century.

Thomas 'Sugar' enters the Montserrat archives only briefly during a police incident where he got shot by mistake, leaving him limping and unsuccessfully seeking recompense from the police. Cassell links her oral interviews with Thomas 'Sugar' to the sketchy police records, combining the official record with the authentic voice. Without this cultural memory, she writes,

> Thomas 'Sugar' remains voiceless in the Archives. [Now] his story has been shared for posterity. It is a story that documents the history of Montserrat and echoes the abject poverty of the labouring classes … highlighting the limited choices for making a living available to the descendants of the formerly enslaved in a society where little provision was made for meaningful education of the masses.
>
> (Cassell, 2018, p. 473)

The story of Thomas Sugar is both a touchstone for the cultural and collective memory of Montserrat and an embodied memory of the island itself, incorporated within the individual and augmented through inscription. Without oral expressions, Thomas 'Sugar' Riley is only an official accident, but with them he is a fully realized person whose voice tells the story of an individual and of a society.

Archives can be powerful social forces. In 2002 Terry Cook and Joan Schwartz galvanized the global archival community when they asserted that archives as social constructs have always been "about maintaining power, about the power of the present to control what is, and will be, known about the past, about the power of remembering over forgetting" (Cook & Schwartz, 2002, p. 3). People and communities are empowered through the legitimizing of their records and their history. But they can also be rendered powerless by the denial of archival legitimacy, by their omission from the archives, and by the marginalization of their narrative.

At its core, this book is about the distribution of archival power. But the distribution of archival power cannot begin to be addressed unless that power is equalized through acknowledging all forms of recording, maintaining and preserving history, memory and collective identity.

Notes

1 The essays in this volume detail the complex technology and multidisciplinary approaches to creating the Circus Oz Living Archive and present the challenges and potential for bringing the archives out of their boxes and files and into a dynamic and fluid digital arena.

2 Quoted in Sabra Statham, "Multimedia Review: John Cage Unbound: A Living Archive, http://exhibitions.nypl.org/johncage/; John Cage: Official Website. http://johncage.org/

References

A People's Archive of Police Violence in Cleveland (2022). *Purpose.* https://www.archivingpoliceviolence.org/

Assmann, A. (2010). Canon and archive. In A. Erll & A. Nünning (Eds.) *A companion to cultural memory studies* (pp. 97–108). De Gruyter.

Brier, S. & Brown, J. (2011). The September 11 digital archive, saving the histories of September 11, 2001. *Radical History Review,* 111, pp. 101–109.

Brugger, N. (2018). *The Archived Web: Doing History in the Digital Age,* MIT Press.

Carlin, D. & Vaughan, L. (2015). Performing digital: An introduction. In D. Carlin & L. Vaughan (Eds.) *Performing digital: Multiple perspectives on a living archive* (pp. 1–10). Ashgate.

Cassell, G. (2018). Capturing personal stories, oral histories and microhistories: A case study from Monserrat. In J.A. Bastian, J.A. Aarons & S.H. Griffin (Eds.) *Decolonizing the Caribbean record: An archives reader* (pp. 461–474). Litwin Books.

Christen, K. (2015). Tribal archives, traditional knowledge, and local contexts: Why the 's' matters. *Journal of Western Archives,* 6(1), pp. 1–21. https://digitalcommons.usu.edu/westernarchives/vol6/iss1/3

Circus Oz Living Archive (2014). https://circusozlivingarchive.com/

Cook, T. & Schwartz, J. (2002). Archives, records, and power: From (post-modern) theory to (archival) performance. *Archival Science,* 2, pp. 171–185.

Documenting the now (n.d.). https://www.docnow.io/

Ham, F.G. (1975). The archival edge. *American Archivist,* 38(1), pp. 5–13.

Jones, M. (2016). Documenting things: Bringing archival thinking to interdisciplinary collaborations. *Australian Library Journal,* 65(3), pp. 213–223.

Kaldor Public Art Projects (2022). *Living archives.* https://kaldorartprojects.org.au/living-archives/

Leprince-Ringuet, D. (2018). *Google's latest experiment teaches AI to dance like a human. Wired.* https://www.wired.co.uk/ article/google-ai-wayne-mcgregor-dance-choreography

McKemmish, S., Chandler, T. & Faulkhead, S. (2019). Imagine: a living archive of people and place "somewhere beyond custody." Archival Science, 19, pp. 281–301.

Miles, A. (2015). 12 Statements for archival flatness. In D. Carlin & L. Vaughan (Eds.) *Performing digital: Multiple perspectives on a living archive* (pp. 39–50). Ashgate.

National Archives of Australia (n.d.). *Discovering Anzacs,* https://discoveringanzacs.naa.gov.au/

New York Public Library (2022). *John Cage unbound: A living archive.* https://www.nypl.org/node/179024

Palka, P. (2020). *The Palka diaries, exile to leeds.* (Video). YouTube https://palkadiaries.co.uk/exile-to-leeds-6/

Roy Rosenzweig Center for History and New Media (2002–2022). *The September 11 digital archive, Saving the histories of September 11, 2001.* https://911digitalarchive.org/

Roy Rosenzweig Center for History and New Media (2021). *Remembering the creation of the September 11 digital archive.* https://rrchnm.org/news/remembering-the-creation-of-the-september-11-digital-archive/

Sabiescu, A.G. (2020). Living archives and the social transmission of memory. *Curator, The Museum Journal,* 63(4), pp. 497–510.

Sassoon, J. (2007). Sharing our story: An archaeology of archival thought. *Archives and Manuscripts,* 35(2), pp. 40–53.

Stanford University Libraries (2022). *Stanford University's living archive of William McDonough.* https://mcdonough.com/stanford-universitys-living-archive-william-mcdonough/

Statham, S. (2015). Multimedia review: John Cage unbound: A living archive, http://exhibitions.nypl.org/johncage/; John Cage: Official Website. http://johncage.org/. *Journal of the Society for American Music,* 9(1), pp. 159–161.

The Living Archive: Extinction Stories from Oceania (n.d.). *About the living archive.* https://www.extinctionstories.org/about-the-living-archive/

Theimer, K. (2015). Digital archives. In L. Duranti & P.C. Franks (Eds.) *Encyclopedia of archival science* (pp. 157–159). Rowman & Littlefield.

UC San Diego Library (2017). What is a living archive. *Tell us how UC it: A living archive,* https://knit.ucsd.edu/tellushowucit/what-is-a-living-archive/

University of Virginia Library (1993–2007). *The valley of the shadow.* https://valley.lib.virginia.edu/

Ward, R.M. (2020, July 25). *Liliuokalani. archival experimentations.* (Video) https://vimeo.com/441699782

Index

Note: Page numbers followed by "n" refer to notes

Acker, A. 45
Alivizatou, M. 18
Alleyne, M. 57
Anderson, K. 35, 48
archival heritage: academic discipline 25; archival turn 25–28; collections 24–25; documentation 26; issue of ownership 24; metaphorical view 28; non-traditional records 28; societal provenance 22; theory 21–22
archival theory 7–9, 12, 21–22, 25, 28
archival thinking 6, 102, 110–112
Ashie-Nikoi, E. D. 32, 33, 41, 54, 55
Assmann, A. 87, 88, 90, 108

Bakhtin, M. 78
Banton, M. 40
Barber, K. 59, 60
Brügger, N. 102
Buckland, M. 4
bullae 37
Burton, A. 58
Butler, B. 13
Butters, S. 62, 63

Cage, J. 107
Calypso 54, 79, 80
Cándida Smith, R. 81
Caribbean Carnival 77–81
carnival in the archives: cultural identity 78; dance 72–74; modeling performance 77–81; performance and provenance 76–77
Cassell, G. 112
Ceja Alcalá, J. 74
Chodorow, S. 32
Circus Oz Living Archive 105–108
Clanchy, M. 64
collective memory 85–87, 97–98
colonialism 13, 24, 26, 39, 40–42, 63, 77, 80, 98
Colwell, C. 4, 46
communities of records 89, 90
community archives: digital community 93; SAADA's mission 93; virtual community 93
Connerton, P. 74, 77, 86, 93
Connolley, I. C. 5, 36
Constitution Act 65
Cook, J. 66
Cook, T. 32, 34, 39, 43, 46, 58, 89, 113
Craith, M. N. 17
cultural archives: challenges of 101; digital archives 102–110; intellectual process 101; memory and community 94–95; overview of 1–4
cultural heritage: archival model 12; broader vision 18–20; characteristics of 20, 29; collective archive 33; folklore 15; intangible 16, 17; monuments to intangible 13–18; tangible 14, 17; UNESCO's efforts 18

cultural memory 9, 18, 60, 84, 85, 87–88, 90, 93–95, 98, 108, 113
Cunningham, A. 28, 67n2

Davis, S. 60, 75
Dearstyne, B. 46
decolonization 42, 48
Delsalle, P. 36, 37, 54, 66
Derrida, J. 25
Desmond, J. 71, 72
Dictionary of Archives Terminology 44, 57
Dictionary of Caribbean English Usage 53
digital archives: born-digital records 103; digital gatherings 108–109; digital interventions 109–110; digital media 102; living archives 103–108; reborn digital media 102, 104
digital technologies 93, 95, 96, 98, 102, 110, 112
Dirks, N. 42
Dunham, K. 72, 73

Eichhorn, K. 27
Eichmann, A. 86
Elders, Y. 94
European imperialism 13

Faulkhead, S. 39, 62
Feith, J. A. 38
finding the record: archives 43–45; records 45; values 46–48
Flinn, A. 91, 93
Fredericksen, C. 63
Fruin, R. 38

Geertz, C. 4
Gilliland, A. 37, 38, 40, 46
Griffin, S. 42, 80

Halbwachs, M. 85, 86, 90
Hall, S. 4, 7, 19
Ham, F. G. 39, 101, 102, 112
Hanks, W. 57, 58
Harris, V. 67n2
Hill, E. 78, 79
History of Archival Practice 54
Hostetter, E. 63
Hunte, J. 72
Hurley, C. 21, 22, 45

intangible cultural heritage 6, 13, 15–18, 94, 95

Jenkinson, H. 38, 44
Jenkinsonian model 58
Jones, M. 111

Kecskeméti, C. 25
Kelly, L. 64
Ketelaar, E. 28, 61, 62, 90
Kuhn, A. 61

Lamming, G. 10
Lemieux, V. 43
Lowenthal, D. 20, 24
Lowry, J. 39
Lubar, S. 45

Mabo v Queensland No. 2 66
The *Manual for the Arrangement and Description of Archives* 38
A Manual of Archive Administration 38, 39
Martin, H.-J. 33
Maze, E. 59
McDonough, W. 107
McGregor, W. 107
McKemmish, S. 47, 102
memory: archives 88–89; collective memory 85–87, 97–98; community 89–92; cultural archives 94–95; cultural memory 87–88, 95; digital technologies 96; text as archive 60–62; texts function 60
Miles, T. 41
Miller, F. 44
Modern Archives: Principles and Techniques 38
Mudimbe, V. Y. 61
Muller, S. 38

Nesmith, T. 22

O'Connor, P. 64
Oke, A. 73, 74
Ong, W. 55, 56, 63
oral archives 54, 66

Orality and Literacy 55
oral traditions: folkstory 53; folktale as text 59–60; living records and memory 55; memory texts 62; oral and the textual 55–59; records 54; written culture 55

Pearce-Moses, R. 45
pictograms 5, 46
Posner, E. 24, 37
Posner's assertion 37

reading the text: landscapes 62–64; memoryscapes 64
recordkeeping 2, 5, 7, 10n1, 21, 33–41, 62, 112
record-making 20, 32–40, 42, 46
reimagining archives 7–8
Rheingold, H. 93
Richards, T. 40
rock art 3, 5, 17, 32, 36
Roebuck, E. 67n1
Rosenzweig, R. 75

Sassoon, J. 110
Schellenberg, T. 38
Schneider, W. 59
Schwartz, J. 43, 113
Scott, D. 27
Selvon, S. 10
Smith, L. T. 48
Smithsonian Folklife Festival 1
South Asian American Digital Archive (SAADA) 93
spoken utterance 55
Statham, S. 113n2
Sturken, M. 60
Sugar, T. 113
Sutherland, T. 56, 72

Taylor, D. 70, 71, 72
text: cultural artifacts 71; folktales as 59–60; memory text 60–62; reading 62–64
Turkel, W. 25, 62

Vansina, J. 53, 65
Voices of Women 33
von Ranke, L. 26

Wareham, E. 6
Western archival frameworks 110
Western archival models 2
Western archival theory 8, 9
Winter, J. 86
Wurl, J. 22

Yeo, G. 4, 34, 35, 37, 45, 47

For Product Safety Concerns and Information please contact our EU
representative GPSR@taylorandfrancis.com
Taylor & Francis Verlag GmbH, Kaufingerstraße 24, 80331 München, Germany

www.ingramcontent.com/pod-product-compliance
Lightning Source LLC
LaVergne TN
LVHW020640100826
845148LV00012B/2271

* 9 7 8 0 3 6 7 5 5 0 7 1 4 *